Rudolf Steiner's Intentions
for the Anthroposophical Society

Rudolf Steiner's Intentions
for the Anthroposophical Society

The Executive Council,
the School for Spiritual Science,
and the Sections

Peter Selg

2011
STEINERBOOKS

SteinerBooks
610 Main Street, Great Barrington, MA 01230
www.steinerbooks.org

Translated by Christian von Arnim.

Originally published in German as *Der Vorstand, die Sektionen und
die Gesellschaft. Welche Hochschule wollte Rudolf Steiner?*
by Ita Wegman Institute for Basic Research into Anthroposophy
Pfeffingerweg 1 A, CH-4144 Arlesheim. © 2011 Verlag des
Ita Wegman Instituts.

Cover image: From a blackboard drawing by Rudolf Steiner,
December 27, 1923. CW 260, Appendix 4, Table VIII.
© Rudolf Steiner Archive, Dornach, Switzerland.

Library of Congress Cataloging-in-Publication Data is available.

ISBN: 978-0-88010-738-9

The aim of the Anthroposophical Society will be to promote and support spiritual research, and that of the School for Spiritual Science to engage in this research itself.[1]

— RUDOLF STEINER[1]

Contents

Foreword

I$_\text{N}$ $_\text{THIS}$ $_\text{YEAR}$ of the 150th anniversary of Rudolf Steiner's birth, amidst radio features, events, lectures, and numerous newspaper reports, as well as a few questionable "biographies," the weekly *Das Goetheanum* of March 4, 2011, published a motion for the annual general meeting on April 16 in which a "vote of no-confidence in the executive council" was proposed, with a call for the executive council as a whole to resign. It was also proposed that a new executive council should be formed by (and out of) the group of present and former section leaders; and include, if necessary, additional members. In their reasoning, the proposers of the motion wrote: "The Anthroposophical Society is in a difficult situation in many of the spheres of its life, into which it has been led over the past few years under the leadership of the executive council."[2] A number of points were then listed as the grounds for the motion of no-confidence, including in the first place the general direction of the Goetheanum under the current leadership body: "For about ten years, many members have noted an increasing externalization, a predominant orientation toward a desired recognition from the non-anthroposophic 'outer world'." The motion then goes on to point out, among other things, that the predominant view of the Goetheanum is a "spiritual service center" from which few or no impulses of its own reach out into the world and which to all intents and purposes does no more than administer the Anthroposophical Society ("Instead of a living representation of anthroposophy, only administration exists"); that core anthroposophic concerns and tasks have been sidelined; that the work of the sections has been restricted through staff reductions ("although the advancement of research in the sections is a main task of the Society"); and that there have been interventions and cut-backs from the center in the sphere of the arts, including many job losses. In contrast, there was hypertrophy in the administrative and executive council apparatus, with six fully paid members of the executive council whose tasks were undefined; but who, nevertheless, had taken upon themselves the assertion of rights and decision-making powers with regard to section matters; and indeed, had massively intervened in them ("Although the School for Spiritual Science with its sections is by its nature 'superior' to the Anthroposophical Society, because this is where research takes place that the Society should support, the executive council of the Society sees itself as manager of the section leaders..."). A description of wrong economic decisions and actions follows, which in the view of the proposers of the motion have contributed to the current financial crisis at the Goetheanum, and have led to a loss of confidence among the members, and a continuing fall in donations.

The timing and form of this motion with its detailed reasoning to remove the executive council as a whole came as surprise to many members of the General Anthroposophical Society. Despite the considerable unhappiness about the situation in Dornach, the motion indisputably addressed key issues and problems that, beyond the current situation at the Goetheanum, directly concern the leadership of the executive council and the School for Spiritual Science in Dornach; and, indirectly, the future path of the Goetheanum and of the General Anthroposophical Society. Fundamental questions about these institutions were seldom raised in the past; and surprisingly, written studies, for example, about Rudolf Steiner's plans for a "School for Spiritual Science" as established (or "reestablished") by him in 1923–24, do not, or hardly, exist—just as there are few detailed studies concerning the development of the Goetheanum and the School after Rudolf Steiner's death. The spirituality of the Christmas Conference, the personalities involved, and the crises of the General Anthroposophical Society have received much attention and some historical documentation in recent years. But this by no means applies to the Goetheanum and the School as such, about which there is almost no literature available apart from introductory texts. Many members equate the School for Spiritual Science with holding or listening to the esoteric class lessons of the First Class. A "meeting of the School for Spiritual Science" in this sense is a meeting of Class members for joint work on mantra or general esoteric questions. There is nothing wrong with that, of course, but we must ask ourselves what Rudolf Steiner really meant when he referred to the civilizational tasks of the "School for Spiritual Science" in Dornach. Furthermore, there is decidedly little to be found in the literature or the documentation coming out of the major Society meetings (such as the annual general meeting or conferences) after Rudolf Steiner's death, and in the eight-and-a-half decades since that time, on the acute question as to whether and how it was and is considered possible at all to continue the School in Dornach *in the spirit he intended, but without his presence*, i.e., maintaining the original, very precise objective he had specified. Nor has a great deal been published hitherto, apart from some contributions of its members, about the possible relevance of the General Anthroposophical Society with regard to the implementation or, indeed, the implementability of the School for Spiritual Science.

Given the current leadership debate and the actual reality of the Goetheanum with its working sections and some outstandingly attended conferences, such questions might possibly be considered of little relevance. But here it should not be forgotten that the attraction of the Goetheanum as the center of the Anthroposophical Society and the principal location of the

School for Spiritual Science; and also the perceived leadership role of the executive council (and the veneration of members toward it); have been derived for many people over a long period of time from the Christmas Conference and the foundation of the School in 1923/24. It was on that basis that Rudolf Steiner provided the "esoteric executive council" with comprehensive authority to act, as we know it. This process happened in the course of a great—and final—effort by Steiner, when decisions had to be made to reorganize the General Anthroposophical Society in a time of historical crises. The question regarding the executive council was therefore directly linked to the question about the Society (and the *situation* of the Society), as was the situation of the School; all members of the executive council when Rudolf Steiner was alive were also the leaders of sections. If we want to understand the basis from which these offices derive their power and authority, we have to look back to the time of Rudolf Steiner; but we must also ask ourselves, what from that time is still deemed to be valid and actually practiced in reality. In fact, Rudolf Steiner linked the "authorization" of the Dornach executive council with extensive obligations and tasks; and it is a key question whether it is these obligations or only the office (and the associated authority) which are still authentic in the individuals and the Society today.

In view of the current crisis in the Society in this year of the 150th anniversary of Rudolf Steiner's birth, it appeared useful to me (beyond any debate about personalities) to set out briefly in a concentrated synopsis the shape of the General Anthroposophical Society and the School for Spiritual Science that, in his own words, Dr. Steiner had in mind in 1923/24. In recent years, I have tried to show in various monographs the intensive way in which Rudolf Steiner worked until his death to develop the School with regard to both the First Class[3] and the Medical Section, which he was able to develop the furthest of all the sections of the Dornach School.[4] He had little time before falling ill in October 1924 to implement his intentions

with regard to the School. As a result of the given circumstances, it was possible for him to set forth the esoteric side of a
field of study only in the field of medicine, with two mantrically
constructed training courses for medical students and doctors;
and to write a spiritual-scientific textbook with the section
leader Ita Wegman. He handed over to Dr. Wegman on March
29, 1925, one day before his death, the corrected first chap-
ter, "True Knowledge of the Human Being as a Foundation for
the Art of Medicine." The book *Extending Practical Medicine:
Fundamental Principles Based on the Science of the Spirit*, which
Ita Wegman published in Dornach in the autumn of 1925, six
months after Rudolf Steiner's death, was the School's first publication for professionals. ("Significant matters have been given
in this book."⁵) One can understand from the development of
the Medical Section in 1924/25 what Rudolf Steiner sought to
achieve with the School; and in what sense he was able to say
that the newly established School for Spiritual Science was (and
is) the "esoteric school of the Goetheanum," divided into various sections. Medicine also shows how Steiner saw the exoteric
representation of esoteric content, and how he perceived the
future work of the Goetheanum—as a School for Spiritual
Science—in the public sphere.

It is not my opinion that the following pages necessarily
contribute direct help or present anything of a decisive nature
to the current crisis in the Society, and that is not my intention.
On the other hand, questions connected with the way that an
office is conducted, along with the relevant personal qualities
and deficits, must also always be seen against a wider background of principle and as an expression (often unspoken) of
the weight accorded to matters of substance. In this respect, it
is expressly to be regretted that open and honest discussions of
principle with the active participation of the membership about
the path of the Goetheanum and the Anthroposophical Society
are seldom held. Under the surface, there is most certainly
an impression that far-reaching decisions about direction are

being made by individuals without being transparently justified; or indeed, subject to discussion in front of—*and with*— the membership (and not merely with delegated "persons in positions of responsibility"). Yet it is absolutely the right time to talk about the future path of the General Anthroposophical Society and its offshoots in the world, of which there are many alongside the Goetheanum in Dornach, particularly as the extent of the crises affecting many of these institutions is no less than in 1923. On closer inspection, it is quite obvious that most of the anthroposophic institutions (or institutions resulting from anthroposophy); including Waldorf schools and curative education homes; and also individual clinics and one anthroposophic medicine producer; are currently facing existential crises. And these crises are not primarily or exclusively financial in nature, but concern their spiritual substance and inner identity; their spirit and what they see as their task; that is, their unique contribution to our culture. Many "anthroposophic" institutions have hardly any anthroposophists left working in them any longer, or even people who have a real interest in anthroposophy, or who work on the basis of the anthroposophic understanding of the human being. It cannot be ignored that many places have only retained the name that bears such promise, without being able or wanting to honor the expectations associated with it—a situation that leads to the misrepresentation of facts, and in reality damages the standing of anthroposophy. Furthermore, with the concern that there are fewer new applicants to the various professional groups, we may well ask whether Dornach, as the headquarters of the General Anthroposophical Society and the School for Spiritual Science, should not direct its attention urgently and with joint responsibility to *such* topics before it is definitively too late for many places. Seen in this light, the given existential and identity problems, as well as the question of truth, by no means concern just the Goetheanum, but the Anthroposophical Society and movement as such. This is something that should not be ignored in view of the current anniversary events and the widely used expression, "Hearing, reading, celebrating and enjoying Steiner."

Perhaps the 150th anniversary of Rudolf Steiner's birth represents an opportunity to reflect once again on his intentions with regard to the School, and the overall significance and tasks of the Goetheanum and the General Anthroposophical Society in our civilization; and to further consider the question as to what relevance his statements, intentions, emphases, and goals should in future have in Dornach and elsewhere. A thoroughly honest answer would be desirable; against it is measured our own behavior, our own contribution to the whole, and perhaps also the "will for the future."

PETER SELG

New York, N.Y. USA
March 2011

Dr. Rudolf Steiner (1861–1925)

1

Rudolf Steiner's Concept of the School for Spiritual Science

Anthroposophy had already found scientifically trained and working members in a whole variety of fields at the time when construction was started; and as there was, therefore, the prospect of applying the methods of spiritual science in the individual sciences, I was able to propose that the building should be given the additional designation "School for Spiritual Science."

— RUDOLF STEINER[6]

T HE FOUNDATION of the School for Spiritual Science, as an internationally active place of anthroposophic research, teaching, and training; and as an outwardly radiating center of forward-looking, culturally influential spirituality; was an intimate part of Rudolf Steiner's life, the real purpose of his work. "The idea of a School for Spiritual Science is the necessary consequence arising from the provision of the spiritual knowledge that our time has been privileged to receive," was how he described it, as early as October 1911.[7] Rudolf Steiner was a thoroughly modest person, at the same time he was aware of the binding obligations that were, and are still, linked with the appearance of anthroposophy at the start of the age of Michael. Despite all the resistance and obstacles inherent in our civilization, the "spiritual knowledge" to which he had acquired access at the beginning of the "light age" belonged out in the open; not just in small esoteric communities, but among the general public. From the start of his work for theosophy and then for anthroposophic spiritual science, Rudolf Steiner placed great value on lectures and writings which were accessible (at least potentially so) to every person. "Our task today is to capture the full flow of spiritual life which, I might say, comes to us from on high."[8] Rudolf Steiner did not want to keep the insights acquired in this way to himself, but was convinced from the beginning that they were required by the present times—even if the anthroposophic viewpoints and perspectives were sometimes vehemently rejected. At stake was to properly fulfill the "great task" of the present, *"which consists of capturing the rays of a new spiritual light that have now become accessible to humanity, and infusing them into the resources of human culture and civilization."* [9]

Rudolf Steiner considered a key place, indeed a decisive place where such an "infusion" of original spiritual-scientific content and perspectives into the world should take place, to be a proper institution (school) of higher learning. He never used this term lightly. Rudolf Steiner would never have given an anthroposophic meeting place, with its lectures, seminars, artistic performances, and conferences, the title of "School for Spiritual Science." On the contrary, he justified his choice of words, which was connected with the Goetheanum in Dornach from the beginning (from 1913), in the following way:

> Anthroposophy had already found scientifically trained and working members in a whole variety of fields at the time when construction was started; and as there was, therefore, the prospect of applying the methods of spiritual science in the individual sciences, I was able to propose that the building should be given the additional designation "School for Spiritual Science" [10]

The foundation stone of the Goetheanum was laid on September 20, 1913. The building was to be an "external monument" for those things "which this spiritual science can incorporate into modern culture." [11] Rudolf Steiner understood such an "incorporation" (or "infusion") in the sense of a scientific center that extended its work to a variety of fields and areas of civilization, and that made its results public. Young academics who were interested in anthroposophy, indeed involved in it, had already approached Rudolf Steiner, even before 1913, and Steiner had hoped and intended that they would come to work in Dornach. He developed the idea of research institutes located in the area surrounding the wooden two-domed building; as well as institutions of public life, including a clinic, in which the spiritual-scientific method was to be *put into practice*. We can be sure that very early on, Rudolf Steiner had his inner eye turned to a great variety of enterprises and associated places of research, application, and training, as was evidenced in the scenes he wrote for his fourth mystery drama (1913). A modern School for Spiritual Science could and should be an attractive location sought out by people for study and training, to extend and deepen their knowledge, and also to deepen self-knowledge.

But less than a year after the foundation stone for the building in Dornach had been laid, the First World War broke out, which fundamentally changed the situation in Central Europe. During the war, the money to continue building mostly disappeared; Rudolf Steiner took part in the work himself, as much as he was able, and made sure the construction went on without interruption, even if many things had to be improvised. The idea or concept of the School had not become obsolete through these destructive events; on the contrary. In Rudolf Steiner's view, the one-sidedness and excesses of the materialistic view of the world and human beings were partly responsible for the catastrophe; and it became the greatest urgency for him to give his time to different perspectives on the understanding of the human being, and on social and scientific life. That is why he had not only repeatedly spoken about the threatening danger before the war, but had also driven construction of the building forward. Repeatedly he had emphasized that, if at all possible, the building should be finished by July 1914. This was something that did not happen. The war broke out in August 1914.

The scope of Steiner's work was limited during the war years. He continued to give public and private lectures, and published various writings; but many things he prepared within himself for the future, for the time when peace would be concluded. Six months before the end of the war, he said in Ulm on April 30, 1918:

[...] In the current catastrophic time, we experience in the most terrible way, as has never happened before in the recorded history of human development, that humanity sees itself placed in a dead-end, a real dead-end. And in all seriousness, humanity will emerge from this dead-end only when it decides to add to physical culture, of which humanity is so proud, the real spiritual culture of the earth's soul for our time and for the immediate future of this physical culture. One can try to resist these endeavors to give the earth a new spirituality as much as one wants; the truth will have to assert itself, whatever the circumstances. Humanity is currently living in a terrible catastrophe. If humanity fails to resolve to incorporate the new spirituality referred to here into itself, these catastrophes will recur time after time, sometimes with only very short intervals. This catastrophe and all its consequences will not be healed with the resources that were already familiar to humanity before it occurred. Anyone who still believes this is not thinking in the spirit of the earthly development of humankind. And the catastrophe will continue, even if it can be bypassed for a few years, until humanity interprets and understands it in the only correct way; that it is a sign that people are turning to the spirit, which must penetrate purely physical life. For many people today this may still be a bitter, because uncomfortable, truth, but it is a truth.[12]

As early as the beginning of the twentieth century, Rudolf Steiner characterized theosophy or anthroposophy as "the spiritual culture of the earth's soul for our time and the near future." He repeatedly pointed out that the positive progress of civilization could not be achieved only through making technology (as the application of natural scientific research) ever more perfect; but that this technology necessarily needed to be supplemented (and penetrated) by spiritual science if it was not to be, for all intents and purposes, dehumanized. The natural-scientific view and its domination of the world required a counterpart, a correcting and regulating influence. But this counterbalance would no longer be provided by philosophy or a general cultural or social science, but only by the cognitive discovery of soul and spiritual fields of reality, forces, and qualities; discoveries that are equal and comparable to those of natural science; that is, that also lead to concrete results and practical implementation. Against this background, the planned School for Spiritual Science was, more than ever, a warning. The theologian Friedrich Rittelmeyer subsequently reported the following words from a conversation with Rudolf Steiner shortly before the end of the First World War:

> In mid-1918, I once said to Steiner, "Dr. Steiner, once the war is over, a research institute should be established in which the attempt is made to understand spiritual-scientific results with the academic resources which are available for that. I already have a few hundred marks, and also a few young academics who would be interested in such a project." Thereupon Steiner placed both his hands on my shoulders and said with a happiness I have seldom seen in him, "Yes, my dear Dr. Rittelmeyer, let us do that." In that moment it was perfectly evident what his concern was.[13]

Rudolf Steiner's great concern was indeed to establish such a school with the associated research institutes. The immediate post-war developments, however, made that difficult; and in the widespread confusion and collapse in 1918/19 there was little evidence of the revised thinking towards a "new spirituality" brought up in Ulm. The endeavors supported by Steiner to introduce social threefolding in Württemberg failed; and in December 1919, he said in Dornach:

> Allow three decades of the kind of teaching being done in our universities, and of thinking about social matters in the

way it is today, and you will have a devastated Europe at the end of those thirty years. No matter how many ideals you set up in one field or another—you can talk until you're blue in the face about the individual demands of particular groups of people; you can talk in the belief that insistent demands do something for the future of humanity; all of those things will be in vain if a change does not occur in the foundation of the human soul; in the thinking about the relationship between this world and the spiritual world. If nothing new is learned in that respect, if there is no new thinking, a moral dilemma will engulf Europe![14]

Rudolf Steiner spoke strongly about the kind of teaching in the "universities" and its consequences for scientific and social life. In fact, the thinking underlying National Socialism was developed in detail many years (indeed, decades) ahead of its physical realization—in the academically widespread, pseudoscientific teachings of eugenics, racial hygiene, and social Darwinism. Rudolf Steiner knew that the scientific content and thinking of the present influences the future. That is why, despite all financial difficulties (in the inflationary post-war years) and staffing problems, he held on to the thought of establishing a School for Spiritual Science in Dornach. Furthermore, he prepared for it in concrete ways from 1919 onward, through comprehensive specialist courses in the fields of education, medicine, and the social and natural sciences. In these courses, Rudolf Steiner not only revealed great spiritual-scientific perspectives and detailed results of his research in the various fields of life; but also he outlined many scientific issues and recommended subjects for doctoral and post-doctoral dissertations. He hoped that his anthroposophic audience and friends would take action. Indeed, the courses were no less than a work program for future research institutes, at least in the fields of science and medicine, which numerous people also understood as such. In Stuttgart, Lilly Kolisko built up on her own initiative (without the support or participation of the

Anthroposophical Society, but to Rudolf Steiner's great joy) a biological research institute in which she continued experimental work on various suggestions made in the courses, and where she produced impressive results. In the more immediate surroundings of the Goetheanum, among other ventures, a scientific research community developed around Ehrenfried Pfeiffer and Guenther Wachsmuth, as well as a pharmaceutical laboratory under Oskar Schmiedel, who soon began to work in close association with Ita Wegman, who had begun her own clinical work in Arlesheim in June 1921. In Stuttgart, preparations were made for another anthroposophic clinic with an associated research institute, which opened in the summer of 1921.

Nevertheless, scientific work, other than that of Rudolf Steiner, progressed relatively slowly in the next few years. The doctors were occupied with their clinical work, and had their hands full with looking after their patients and building up the necessary therapeutic structures; and, as well, the most scientifically gifted of the anthroposophists had been asked by Rudolf Stei¬ner himself to work in the new Waldorf school in Stuttgart, in order to give the students an excellent education, and give public proof of the quality of Waldorf education. The faculty of teachers had an unusually high academic standard (which even the Stuttgart education committee noticed), and gave various public lectures and seminars in collaboration with Steiner, which were rightly designated as "higher education courses." Relatively little scientific talent was left over for Dornach, and also little money. The opening weeks of the Goetheanum in the autumn of 1920, which included contributions from many anthroposophic academics, did not impress Rudolf Steiner from a scientific point of view. He referred to a "*Mixtum compositum* of anthroposophy and science"[15] and clearly felt that many anthroposophically-oriented academics placed anthroposophy alongside their specialist knowledge; that is, they understood it as an "extension," without realizing that an inner transformation of the subject had not yet taken place. What was really needed was a transformation of the individual disciplines at their core, and not additive supplementation. Rudolf Steiner also experienced arrogance among the speakers, with considerable overestimation of their own capabilities. In fact, they had not been very innovative or productive in their subjects, but polemicized about conventional "materialism" in the sciences without (as Rudolf Steiner had wanted) entering into a critical and constructive dialogue with other interested academics. Steiner's suggestions and indications in the specialist courses had so far hardly been taken up; and basically little specific and successful scientific activity was evident, other than his lectures (and the devoted work of Lilly Kolisko), that even came close to justifying the claim of a "School for Spiritual Science." Furthermore, Rudolf Steiner did not notice much understanding about Dornach's specific concern among the general membership of the Anthroposophical Society. Most of the members saw the imposing building as an ideal lecture, event, and stage venue; a place at which it would be a pleasure to meet each other, attend the lectures of Rudolf Steiner, the artistic performances in eurythmy, drama, and creative speech under the direction of Marie Steiner; but they did not have a feeling for the urgent needs of the times; or, indeed, the farther-reaching, selfless awareness of a significant anthroposophic input into our civilization. Later, in a bitter review of the years after 1918, Rudolf Steiner said, "What I actually wanted to achieve was continually blunted by the [Anthroposophical] Society; and its power of impulse was taken from it."[16] The destruction through arson of the Goetheanum by opponents of anthroposophy on New Year's eve 1922/23 was seen by Steiner almost as being symbolic of a society that had failed to find itself and its tasks— without even noticing it.

*

Yet Rudolf Steiner did not give up. He tried everything in his power to trigger a "self-reflection" process in the Anthroposophical Society in 1923, an awareness of the problems among the members with regard to the situation affecting civilization as a whole and the significance of anthroposophy within it; and thus also of Dornach and the School for Spiritual Science. The Goetheanum building had been totally destroyed, but Rudolf Steiner's intentions had not. Its reconstruction in concrete was possible and sensible—*if* the community wished to get a grip and actively face the future.[17]

Although Rudolf Steiner was left, at best, with an ambivalent attitude toward the various assemblies, conferences, and crisis meetings of 1923 (a true reorganization and fitness for the future was hardly evident) he finally decided twelve months after the fire not only in favor of a monumental new building for the Goetheanum, but also to take on the chairmanship of the Society himself (up to that time he had not even been a member, but only an independent spiritual teacher). Steiner assumed the leadership after "hard inner resistance";[18] and with the intention of trying his utmost once more in a critical time for civilization (it was eight weeks since Hitler's first Putsch attempt in Germany) to make the School for Spiritual Science a reality.

> If we look at the world today, extraordinarily destructive substance has been evident for some years. Forces are at work that give an inkling of the depths to which western civilization will still sink.[19]

Rudolf Steiner also took on the chairmanship in order, as he said, to be able to determine the "style" in which anthroposophy would be represented in the future from the Goetheanum through the Anthroposophical Society (and its leadership)—in such a way "as I would like to have anthroposophy represented by the Anthroposophical Society."[20] Rudolf Steiner had considered the leadership style of those responsible in the preceding years as decidedly inadequate, and in no way appropriate for the circumstances and problems of the times ("then must anthroposophy as reflected in the Anthroposophical Society be most likely totally misunderstood by the world"[21]). Rudolf Steiner wanted anthroposophic spiritual science in future to be courageously, actively, and directly articulated. He thought little of "public relations work," a term which he neither used nor thought appropriate. Working on public opinion or self-promotion was precisely what was to be avoided. On the contrary, the Goetheanum would make its contribution to public life and to the world by its presence through scientific and artistic contributions, which would be both authentic and of a high level. In the future, Dornach was no longer to be about advertising, Steiner said, but about productive work from a spiritual center, that is, from spiritual sources, without compromise and without any borrowing from anywhere else:

> Take all the things that have flowed into eurythmy. Don't you think that there were not many people who again and again whispered into our ears that here we have something very similar; and there we have something quite similar; we have to take this into account; and that must be integrated. The only way to make productive progress was not to look to left or right; but only to work out of the sources of the subject itself—only out of the sources of the subject itself. If something of a compromise had been introduced, the subject would no longer have been what it is, could not have become what it is. It is part of the conditions of life of such a movement that it is absolutely certain that the things that need to be obtained can be obtained from constantly broadening sources.[22]

If we keep asking: what do we have to do to make ourselves acceptable for some particular group in the world that is not fond of us? How do we have to behave in this field or that so that we are taken seriously here or there? Then we most certainly will not be taken seriously. We will only be taken seriously if at all times we feel through our actions that we have a responsibility toward the spiritual world; if we know that the spiritual world wants something of humanity at the current moment of historical development; wants that something in all the different fields of life; and that it is up to us to follow the impulses from the spiritual world clearly and truthfully. Even if we initially cause offense, in the long term it will be the only thing that is beneficial. And that is why we will also not get along among ourselves unless we are filled at every opportunity with what can come as impulses from the spiritual world.[23]

Our appearance everywhere must be in full truth, whatever the field, as representatives of the being of anthroposophy in the world; and we must become aware that to the extent we cannot do that, we cannot in reality further the anthroposophic movement. All veiled support for the anthroposophic movement does not, in the end, produce anything positive.[24]

The only thing to do is to tell the world the things that have to be said from the anthroposophic center, and then to wait and see how many people have an understanding of it.[25]

Steiner demanded true knowledge of anthroposophy and its content from those who were to work from and for the Goetheanum; he demanded courage and the readiness to take a stand in the world with anthroposophy, and not with a vague "spirituality" without boundaries; the "courage to be wakeful," "courage to be committed."[26] What mattered was the "indication of full truth" and representing the "nature of anthroposophy," and nothing else—even if it meant personal risks or social exclusion and defamation:

> [...] What matters is to have so much inner security with regard to anthroposophy that one is in a position to really represent anthroposophy wherever one is in the world.[27]

Rudolf Steiner knew that the coming years and decades in Central Europe would be difficult and dangerous. The "destructive substance" of which he had spoken was not a metaphor. He knew that the people who would advocate and take responsibility for anthroposophic medicine, education, and curative education would assume great personal risk, including possible persecution. Rudolf Steiner was certain, however, that the difficulties in the world with their very concrete potential for destruction, urgently called for a different image of the human being; and that the greatest service one could do for civilization was to place a clear emphasis on resistance *through* spiritual scientific work; through research, teaching, and one's own life. The Goetheanum as a School for Spiritual Science was intended to be active in the world, to face up to it, and to respond to the problems and challenges from the core of anthroposophy with a selfless view of the existing dangers, "living alongside the destiny of the times."

> The misery that can be seen in civilization today should be seen as a challenge to adopt a suprasensory view of the human being and the world. But we can do that only if we have an open eye for all that is happening in the world.[28]

Particularly in view of the approaching catastrophes (the "misery" of civilization), the Christmas Foundation Meeting and the "refounding" of the Anthroposophical Society, which Rudolf Steiner undertook on that occasion, were of critical importance as the prerequisite for the possible "entry" of the "spirit that humanity needs."[29] "However, esoteric insight reveals that a wave of spiritual science must flood across Europe if there is to be a thorough improvement of life in Europe."[30]

*

Rudolf Steiner made clear in the months after the fire that the Anthroposophical Society was largely incapable of functioning;

it existed without any real awareness of problems and tasks of
the times, and many of its "representatives" lived in complacent
hubris.

Anthroposophy as such was effective and had "punch" ("we
do not need to be concerned about the 'punch' of anthroposophy,
my dear friends"[31]); but a key factor in the given time and world
situation was that the anthroposophic community should recog-
nize its tasks, and allow anthroposophy to take effect through its
activities. ("The main thing is that the Anthroposophical Society
should understand what its obligations are."[32]) It was necessary,
Rudolf Steiner said, that the Anthroposophical Society should
become a "reality" in the future—the near future—which it had
not been in 1923 (and the previous years) "because no positive task arose from a positive intention."[33] Steiner expressly
rejected a community or association exclusively for the study
of anthroposophy, in view of the given contemporary circumstances. On the contrary, it was the duty of anthroposophists
(that is, people who knew about modern spiritual science and
had connected themselves with it as their destiny) to take on
"positive tasks" in the world, tasks "that people out there can
also respect."[34] It was a matter of the "active content" of social
cohesion and the promotion of humanistic values and real goals
with the intention of directing the world "toward the good"
(Schiller). The Anthroposophical Society should express its
commitment to anthroposophy; to anthroposophy's understanding of the human being and the world; and actively promote its
content; that is, "represent the anthroposophic cause before the
whole world in the most forceful way [...]";[35] and thus makes
its stance clear "so that it stands in the world as such, and the
world at last knows what the Anthroposophical Society as such
is about."[36] In 1923/24 there were Waldorf schools in Stuttgart,
Hamburg, and Cologne, as well as two anthroposophic clinics and various other institutions that had come out of anthroposophy, and were able to introduce anthroposophic spiritual
content into the world. They represented a new humanistic,

social approach and ethics of which the times were urgently in need. The Anthroposophical Society as such did not in any real sense evince any responsibility toward these institutions, as to whether they sank or swam, although they were economically under threat and much criticized. The leading anthroposophists, who occupied management functions in the Society, sat on their "curule seats"[37] without seeming to care about either the needs of the times or these young, struggling, socially relevant institutions. That could not continue, as Rudolf Steiner had made clear already in the period before the Christmas Foundation Meeting. The dangers and threats were of an existential nature—not just for the institutions that had been established, but for western civilization itself. Fascism and the total transformation of civilization through technology were already knocking at the door in Central Europe:

> [...] Our time, our present time (and please take this with all seriousness) is a time of great decisions. Many things, terrible things will come to a head for humanity. The present time will of course last for a long time; but many things, immense things, are coming to a head in the present time for humanity.[38]

In this situation the Anthroposophical Society and its center in Dornach had to develop into something "which can have its say in the present,"[39] or it had to dissolve itself; and then anthroposophy would have to pursue another path, beyond the Society.

Rudolf Steiner decided to make one last attempt. He assumed the chairmanship of the Society and appointed a leadership body at the center of which he stood, and with which he intended to tackle the tasks. He did so at great personal risk, but he did not see any other way of still making the Dornach School a reality in the given time and world situation. For a long time Steiner had placed his hope in the initiative of other people closely connected with anthroposophy. Now the reality was that he took action himself, and appointed personalities of great spiritual and professional caliber, with whom he could work and carry out his intentions. The new executive council, described by him as "esoteric," was intended to work "directly out of the substance of the spiritual life"[40] in the future and to take initiative; "it must be an initiative executive council; it must grasp the tasks that the spiritual world has set the anthroposophic movement; must take them up, must guide them into the world, must not just be an administrative council."[41] "It must be an initiative executive council that makes happen what should flow through the Anthroposophical Society as its being."[42] But the target of this whole development was not the Anthroposophical Society as such, its administration and "maintenance"; on the contrary, it was about bringing the impulses of the spiritual world in the age of Michael into the Anthroposophical Society, and through it into civilization in the sense that had long been pursued by Rudolf Steiner. The "General Anthroposophical Society" reestablished in Dornach, was to be a world society and to work comprehensively in the public sphere. Not through press releases, photo features, and interviews, but through convincing specialty academic work. "To this end it [the executive council] is called upon to transfer what is anthroposophic teaching into anthroposophic work in every respect."[43]

All the people who had been appointed at the Christmas Foundation Meeting to work with Rudolf Steiner on the executive council were thus responsible for an area of life; that is, a "section" (faculty) of the Dornach School. Steiner set up only those sections for which he had outstanding personalities at hand; people who performed exceptional work in their field, and who were able also to establish a position in the world through their work. Marie Steiner was highly qualified in the stage arts, Ita Wegman as a doctor and hospital director, Albert Steffen as a widely recognized writer. Because these personalities were well known to Steiner, he was able to establish faculties in the School for them, of which they became the leaders. ("Here we

will not proceed in an abstract way but will proceed by taking
the existing activities to set up the sections from the actual areas
that already exist, from what we already have."[44]) Furthermore,
in Elisabeth Vreede, Rudolf Steiner had an outstanding math-
ematician and astronomer who had also shown in the "School
courses" she had held, that she was well able to initiate and
represent the results of anthroposophic work in her subject;
and that she possessed a strong will and future potential. ("Dr.
E. Vreede works untiringly to introduce anthroposophy into
the field of mathematical sciences."[45]) There are many indications that Rudolf Steiner would have liked to have given the
Natural Science Section of the School for Spiritual Science to
Lilly Kolisko; but she had commitments in Stuttgart and was
not available for the development of the School on the Dornach
hill. In her place, Rudolf Steiner appointed the young active
Guenther Wachsmuth, with whom he had collaborated closely
in the previous years in the field of research into the formative
forces; and for whom he also had great hopes. Rudolf Steiner
intended to lead the Anthroposophical Society and the School
for Spiritual Science from Dornach with this group of people;
thereby, it was understood that all the members of the esoteric
executive council would remain in their previous fields of
work; that is, perform and fill their previous roles as before. Ita
Wegman continued to direct her clinic and the facilities associated with it; Marie Steiner the Dornach stage and the eurythmy
ensemble, which performed in many countries. Albert Steffen
continued to work as a writer and was responsible, to Steiner's
great satisfaction, for the weekly *Das Goetheanum*. With regard
to Vreede and Wachsmuth, too, Steiner undoubtedly had other
tasks in the vicinity of the Goetheanum in mind, in the sense
of research institutes and associated facilities. He did not want
an "administrative executive council," but concrete carriers
of initiatives in the leading positions, who were to ensure that
anthroposophy would become effective and visible in key areas
of life. The outer was to be penetrated by the inner, the exoteric

tasks by the esoteric center of anthroposophy. Even four weeks before the Christmas Foundation Meeting, the then Director Denzler of ILAG, the precursor of what subsequently became Weleda, had written to Rudolf Steiner: "For the successful sale of our preparations under the great competition we face today, the idea must for the time being be relegated to the background. The preparations must be marketed as successful new medicines and special products, and must not be sold as being the result of anthroposophic science; because otherwise doctors will be suspicious and we will never reach a wider public."[46] Rudolf Steiner clearly rejected such an approach and attitude at the Christmas Foundation Meeting:

> Anthroposophy will most certainly remain fruitless in medicine and treatment if there is a tendency in the medical operations within the anthroposophic movement to push anthroposophy as such into the background; and to represent the medical part, for example, of our cause, in such as way that we please those who represent medicine from today's perspective. We must include anthroposophy with great courage in every single thing, including medicine.[47]

In this spirit, all the specialist areas were in future to be represented in the world from the center of anthroposophy. They were to work in this way—and only in this way—with courage, with directness, and without false compromises.

*

After the Christmas Foundation Meeting, Rudolf Steiner himself led the General Anthroposophical and the Pedagogical Sections; additionally, he was the spiritual leader of the Stuttgart Waldorf School, to which he was also fully committed. At the same time, he intended to work intensively with all the Dornach section leaders in their respective subjects. In fact, Rudolf

Steiner's concept of the sections provided for intensive collaboration between the respective section leader and himself, as the real center of initiation of the School; at its core the sections were esoteric working groups composed of Steiner and the leaders appointed by him. Such a structure was necessary, and was grounded in the nature of the School itself. The specialist sections were to undertake genuine scientific research; that is, to work on the methodological basis for the acquisition of spiritual-scientific knowledge in their fields; and in so doing, to achieve tangible results:

> The aim of the Anthroposophical Society will be to promote and support spiritual research; and that of the School for Spiritual Science to engage in this research itself.[48]

Rudolf Steiner's involvement was imperative in order to achieve this goal; therefore, he announced, at the Christmas Foundation Meeting, that he would lead the sections through their leaders. He did not, however, consider it sensible or necessary to report in greater detail about the intended work of the sections at the annual general meeting. "The sections will be structured to work here. We do not really need to talk about the sections at all. They will be founded as they must be founded, in accordance with their work," he emphasized on December 31, 1923, one year after the fire.[49] "From Dornach will come forth what needs to come forth. Out of anthroposophy itself we will certainly find the most precise scientific methods and guidelines."[50] It became clear, or there were at least signs at the Christmas Foundation Meeting, that Rudolf Steiner considered the actual work of the sections to be an internal matter; spiritual research work in the specialist fields, which took place neither in the public view nor in the view of the Anthroposophical Society. Rudolf Steiner had worked with Marie Steiner intensively for a long time in the field of creative speech, drama, and eurythmy; and with Ita Wegman for a long time in the field of medicine.

This research work was to be made visible to the members of the Society (and the public) through its results on the stage, in clinical treatments, in published textbooks; but not through the spiritual inner space of the research itself. The way in which such initiate research can be undertaken in each subject, in collaboration between the teacher and the esoteric pupil, was explained by Rudolf Steiner in principle in the summer of 1924, in Torquay in England, using the example of his medical collaboration with Ita Wegman (at least to those members who wanted to understand it).[51]

In this way, Rudolf Steiner conceived or intended the sections as fields of activity for spiritual-scientific research within a small esoteric community in a dual relationship between himself and the leader of each section. Around this center of specialist research and teaching, groups of people were then intended to form social connections with a professional focus. Interested people willing to commit themselves; who wanted to include the results of the Goetheanum research in their work, and train themselves further in specific training courses; were invited to join the center of the section in Dornach, the place of spiritual-scientific research and teaching. These groups of people (as active members of the School) were of prime importance for spreading the cultural impulse flowing from the Goetheanum; through them the inner esoteric core of the section would spread out into the world. In the closing words of one course, Rudolf Steiner commented on his collaboration with Ita Wegman, who formed the "center" of the Medical Section at the Goetheanum, and on the associated community of "young doctors":

> In this spirit, my dear friends, let us stay united; let us stay united in such a way that you retain your center in Dornach here at the Goetheanum, and really keep to this center, so that this center can work in the world through you.[52]

Against this background, which is important to understand, Rudolf Steiner was able to describe the School that was refounded at the Christmas Foundation Meeting as an "esoteric institution"; that is, the core of the sections, Rudolf Steiner's spiritual-scientific research activity in collaboration with the section leaders, was in itself esoteric in nature.[53]

*

As the supporting pillar for the Dornach School structure, Rudolf Steiner further established an "esoteric school of the Goetheanum"; a spiritual training course methodologically structured as three classes, for which all members of the Anthroposophical Society could register or apply. The increasingly externalized attempts at establishing an "institution of higher education" of the previous years were given a clear rebuff by Rudolf Steiner with the Christmas Foundation Meeting; a "School for Spiritual Science" could be established and justified in our current civilization only as a truly spiritual center. The Anthroposophical Society and the Goetheanum in Dornach had to find and grasp their own inner substance, as the prerequisite for any forward-looking activity in the world.

> The core of [the] esoteric work of the Anthroposophical Society now has to be the esoteric school; that esoteric school which out of the whole character of anthroposophy now has to take the place of what was previously attempted as the so-called School for Spiritual Science; and what cannot be described as having been altogether successful. That was at a time when I had not yet taken over the leadership of the Anthroposophical Society myself; and I therefore had the task of allowing those who wanted to try something, to do so. That can no longer happen in the future. It is part of what was formed in connection with me in the Christmas Foundation Meeting impulse, that the School for Spiritual Science with its various sections now

has to form an esoteric core for all, which in turn is to work esoterically in the Anthroposophical Society.[54]

[...] That is the reason why the School for Spiritual Science was founded at Christmas: so esoteric life would return to our Anthroposophical Society.[55]

The Christmas Foundation Meeting indicated that if the Anthroposophical Society is to develop its activity in the right way in future, it has to leave the paths that it pursued in recent years; it must reach for the inner spiritual from the outer business-like. It must as a whole assume an esoteric character. What will exist in the future in Dornach as the School for Spiritual Science must bear a kind of esoteric character, and the whole institution of the Society must bear an esoteric character. That will give the Society the spiritual life it needs. It must not become externalized, and that is the threat it was under in recent years.[56]

Rudolf Steiner considered that the sections of the Dornach School belong to the "esoteric school of the Goetheanum." The esoteric movement in the narrower sense was "structured" into various sections[57] and was "nuanced" into the individual specialist areas. Rudolf Steiner held his training course for the "First Class" within the General Anthroposophical Section from February 15, 1924, onward; this section was to "contain the esoteric substance for all human souls";[58] whereas within the specialist sections, training events would in future be held with specific occupational relevance. How he intended to carry out esoteric training events in the individual sections for the members of the School associated with them (and what he understood, in concrete terms, by the social being of a section) Rudolf Steiner was able to demonstrate in the Medical Section, during the two mantrically structured training courses for medical students and young doctors which were held in January and April 1924.[59] In this connection, it is also of interest that Rudolf Steiner described the medical *Newsletter* for the participants of the course, which contained answers from him and Ita Wegman to questions that had been asked, as a report about the "continuing work of the School";[60] that is, he indicated in this way once again that the actual work of the School was esoteric research work that took place at the center of the "School for Spiritual Science" and extended into the various specialist areas. The institutions of anthroposophy already existing in the world were also to benefit from that in the future, which is why Rudolf Steiner especially welcomed it when all the members of the faculty of teachers of the Stuttgart school joined the Dornach School (as Class members). He favored their affiliation with Dornach not (just) as private persons, but as the faculty of teachers; that is, in their capacity as teachers of the independent Waldorf School; and he made clear that in this way the impulse of the Dornach School would be able to penetrate the educational work of the Waldorf school even more deeply than before.[61]

*

Rudolf Steiner refounded the Dornach School in 1923/24. He said in general terms:

> [...] Here in Dornach there must be a place where, for those who want to find out about it, all the important, direct events in the spiritual world can be spoken about. Here must be a place where the strength is found, not just to indicate in the endless, dialectically materialistic scientific approach of the present, that there might be minute traces of something spiritual here or there. If Dornach is to fulfill its task, then people must be able to find out here openly what is happening in the spiritual world in historical terms; what is happening in the spiritual world as impulses that then enter natural existence and govern nature; they must be able to find out in Dornach about real experiences, about real forces, about real beings of the spiritual world. This is where the school of real spiritual science must be.[62]

However, Rudolf Steiner said that this also applied in principle to the various areas of life. Starting from the Dornach center, which was to exercise a spiritualizing and activating function for the General Anthroposophical Society, the Society was in future to introduce anthroposophy into the world in a 'healing' way with the assistance of *all* those anthroposophists who felt at home in the newly founded body. At the end of the Christmas Foundation Meeting, Rudolf Steiner bade the members of the General Anthroposophical Society farewell with the words: "So, my dear friends, take away with you your warm hearts in which you have laid the foundation stone for the Anthroposophical Society; take away with you your warm hearts *to act with strength and healing in the world.*"[63]

The "esoteric school of the Goetheanum," he said, was to become the "heart" and "soul" of the newly formed Anthroposophical Society, aware of its global tasks and global responsibility. The Christmas Foundation Meeting was not to be a "list of pious hopes,"[64] but an impulse to take action. Rudolf Steiner worked toward this with all his strength, right up to the time he fell ill, nine months after the Christmas Foundation Meeting. On May 25, 1924, he commented in Paris on the medical textbook he wrote with Ita Wegman:[65]

This [spiritual-scientific] quality will now enter medicine from Dornach through the efforts of Dr. Wegman and myself in a book that is about to be published, that speaks freely of the things esoteric knowledge can contribute to medicine. That is also what forms the basis of the Christmas Foundation Meeting [...] as its most profound impulse.[66]

Rudolf Steiner wanted to work in this way not just with Ita Wegman, but with all the other section leaders as well, to research jointly, work jointly, and publish jointly on the spiritual-scientific foundations for a new theory of words, language, and movement; on physics, chemistry, biology, agriculture, mathematics, and astronomy; and also on anthroposophic aesthetics and related subjects based on spiritual science. A first meeting with farmers working on the basis of anthroposophy was to take place in Dornach at the end of September 1924. They had received new foundations for their work in the agriculture course given by Steiner at Whitsun in Koberwitz, and since then had been gathering their experiences on their farms. Guenther Wachsmuth had been in contact with them, and Lilly Kolisko had achieved impressive results in Stuttgart in her experiments with various indications from the course. However, the intended meeting on September 27 never happened because Rudolf Steiner was ill, critically ill. This would change many things, indeed almost everything.

Few things were possible in the coming months. During the time of Steiner's illness, Elisabeth Vreede attempted to get the publication on Rudolf Steiner's specialist astronomical course underway with her collaborator Wilhelm Kaiser; she received Steiner's approval for the book (*Astronomy as elucidated by spiritual science*. Dornach, 1925). Albert Steffen was able to have a few last conversations with the teacher on artistic and literary issues; the forms for eurythmy performances were created on Steiner's sickbed. Until almost the very last moment, Rudolf Steiner was considering questions regarding the interior design of the new Dornach building. But then, on the morning of March 30, 1925, fifteen months after the Christmas Foundation Meeting (and after the start of the School, which had hardly even begun to get underway), everything came to an abrupt end; a tragic event with untold consequences.

Rudolf Steiner had been in a hurry to establish the School for Spiritual Science. He knew that time was running out; he was aware of the precarious and crisis-ridden state of the Anthroposophical Society, and the growing problem of the historical situation. At the Christmas Foundation Meeting he had once more asked Lilly Kolisko to give a comprehensive account of her research into "the properties of smallest entities" (which had been largely ignored by leading representatives of the Anthroposophical Society in Stuttgart and the college of physicians at the Stuttgart clinic). Afterward, her report, on the anniversary of the fire, had been sent out to all the members of the Anthroposophical Society who had been present at the Meeting.

Now, my dear friends, you have seen that we are quietly working on the scientific problems, and that it is indeed possible to give a stimulus to science on the basis of anthroposophic research in the way that is truly needed today. And those things are really possible at this time (I mean at this time in the anthroposophic movement), only because there are such dedicated workers who devote themselves to the matter at hand in such a selfless way, as for example Dr. Kolisko. Perhaps, in the course of time, when you reflect on the matter, you will be able to appreciate the huge amount of work that was required to determine all these sequential data that give these results, which are then reproduced in this clear curve.

But all these experiments are basically, particularly from an anthroposophic perspective, individual parts of a totality; a totality that is scientifically so urgently required today. And if our work continues, as it has been done so far in our research institute, then we will perhaps have achieved in fifty or seventy-five years what needs to be achieved: that many individual elements combine into a totality. This totality will then be of great significance not just with regard to our knowledge, but also for the whole of our practical life.

People have no idea today how deeply all these things can intervene in practical life; intervene in the making of the products people need, intervene specifically in treatment methods, and similar things. Now, you might say that human progress has always been slow, and why should anything be different in this field? But it might well be that, given the present brittle state of our current civilization, its openness to destruction, we would not find the connection in fifty or seventy-five years to still be able to do what it is absolutely necessary to do. And in this context I might be allowed to say, not as a wish, not even as a possibility, but only as what I might call a fantasy: that those things which could be achieved in fifty to seventy-five years if they continue at the speed with which we are forced to work (and which indeed are achievable in that time only through such dedicated staff as Dr. Kolisko, for example), that those things could also be done in five or ten years. I am convinced that if we were able to create the necessary tools and the necessary institutes, and have more staff who would work in this spirit, we would be able to do in five or ten years what would otherwise take about fifty to seventy-five years. The only other thing we would require for such work would be about 50 to 75 million francs. We would indeed then perhaps be able to do the work in a tenth of the time. As I said, I do not present this as a wish, not as a possibility, but only as a fantasy—but a very real fantasy. If we had the 75 million francs, we would indeed be able to do what it is absolutely necessary to do. That is something which might at least be considered.[67]

These remarks give an indication of what was at stake with the success or failure of the School for Spiritual Science in terms of our civilization, and also the kind of concrete support that Rudolf Steiner hoped for in the following period from the Anthroposophical Society. ("But it might well be that given the present brittle state of our current civilization, its openness to destruction, we would not find the connection in fifty or seventy-five years to still be able to do what it is absolutely necessary to do.") It also becomes comprehensible why Rudolf Steiner wrote in the statutes of the newly founded General Anthroposophical Society: "The aim of the Anthroposophical Society will be to promote and support research in the spiritual domain, and that of the School for Spiritual Science to engage in this research itself."

*

Rudolf Steiner: Model of the Second Goetheanum (1924)

2

Developments, Questions, and Perspectives

And so the ways and means must be found to engage in more anthroposophy, or in other words, to present anthroposophy to the world in such a way that its own quality prevents the defamations of opponents from harming it. Ways and means must be found to continue what was intended from the very beginning for anthroposophy.

— RUDOLF STEINER[69]

T HE DEATH of Rudolf Steiner on March 30, 1925, did not mark the end of the history of the School for Spiritual Science. Steiner's closest collaborators, his colleagues in the executive council, believed that to a limited extent they could (and indeed, should) through their own resources continue to develop and lead the School envisaged by their teacher. Although they had doubts about their own capacities to do so; and although they were sufficiently aware that the School could no longer be a center of initiation and research without Rudolf Steiner; they trusted that their attempt to continue the work corresponded to his intentions. Dr. Steiner had established the School in the very last phase of his life, in clear awareness of the fact that his personal involvement in it on earth would be brief; even if, in all likelihood, he did not know how brief. He undertook its future-oriented founding with the optimism he had cultivated over a lifetime, relying on his capable, productive, and creative colleagues, to whom he promised his help, both in Dornach and further afield.

In many of his anthroposophical lectures, Steiner had spoken about the activities of the "dead," those who had departed from the earth; and of the possibilities of establishing a relationship and connection with them as the basis for receiving help from other spheres of existence. Indeed, during his life, Steiner himself successfully undertook and realized a great deal with the help of the "dead."[70] In this sense, the connection between Rudolf

Steiner and his colleagues on the "esoteric executive council," who had a deep, spiritual relationship with him, could continue both as individuals and as a community. The term "esoteric executive council" (later increasingly disparaged) was certainly taken most seriously by him: the whole schooling of the "First Class," for which the executive council bore responsibility, made possible a real connection with the world of spirit and the beings at work in it; and, as a process of communion, also with the individuality who had once brought the Class Lessons to earth and taught them.[71]

All of the executive council members tried to keep alive in themselves, in their work, and in their sections, the spiritual-scientific bases and methods of their specialist fields, and an ongoing sense of their close bond with the spiritual figure of Rudolf Steiner. Marie Steiner, Ita Wegman, Albert Steffen, Elisabeth Vreede, and Guenther Wachsmuth continued to work, and as far as they were able, to develop their specialist sections; and in this they were successful. From the outset, the spheres of activity of Ita Wegman and Marie Steiner were international in scope: in the medical and therapeutic fields, and in eurythmy and creative speech, working groups were formed with a connection to the sections in Dornach. Well-attended public lectures and events, as well as artistic performances, took place in European cities; and internal training and advanced training courses were held in Dornach and Arlesheim that further explored the work of Rudolf Steiner in relation to specific professions. All this was fruitful in a practical way. Along with her commitment to the section she led; to managing the stage work; and to her position on the executive council, Marie Steiner worked on publishing the collected works of Rudolf Steiner, including all his books and lecture cycles. Elisabeth Vreede, too, in the context of the "Rudolf Steiner Archive at the Goetheanum," accomplished outstanding work. Vreede's aim was to make accessible Rudolf Steiner's vast lecturing oeuvre as the School's spiritual core to all the professional groups and interested people, with the addition of indexes, annotations, and references that she would provide. Over and above this, in Vreede's competently edited Section journals, she published Rudolf Steiner's indications and the tasks proposed by him in the fields of mathematics and astronomy.[72] Albert Steffen continued to take overall responsibility for the weekly *Das Goetheanum*, and endeavored to ensure that the central news publication of the Anthroposophical Society *and* of the School for Spiritual Science remained at a high standard, in line with Rudolf Steiner's vision. Along with responsibility for the Natural Science Section, Guenther Wachsmuth took overall responsibility for the construction of the second Goetheanum as the School's central location. On the magnificent stage there, Marie Steiner directed extraordinary productions of Rudolf Steiner's mystery plays, as well as plays by, among others, Albert Steffen, whose work as a writer continued despite all time constraints and was an important part of the School.

Marie Steiner, Ita Wegman, Albert Steffen, Elisabeth Vreede, and Guenther Wachsmuth all knew that however great their commitment to their work, they would never reach the level of achievement they had formerly accomplished with Rudolf Steiner. None of them ever claimed to be able to research and teach in the spiritual-scientific way that Rudolf Steiner had done. Dr. Steiner had said, "From Dornach will come what needs to come. Out of anthroposophy itself we will certainly find the most precise scientific methods and guidelines." Now he was no longer there to support them in their professional work, which (at the level of spiritual research by an initiate) could not be accomplished without him. It was impossible to deceive oneself about this, and no one did so. Marie Steiner, Ita Wegman, Albert Steffen, Elisabeth Vreede, and Guenther Wachsmuth also knew that none of them had the spiritual capacity to establish the Second or Third Class of the Esoteric School; nor even (beyond the medical courses given in January and April 1924) to take the first steps through their own resources of developing and implementing a profession-specific mantric training at the level of the School for Spiritual Science. Nevertheless, they continued to work, preserving and furthering what had been given by Steiner. They looked ahead with a sense of responsibility toward anthroposophy and their spiritual teacher; and also toward the people who were working in the world in the various initiatives and groups that had formed while Rudolf Steiner was alive—and who hoped for support from Dornach, from the School for Spiritual Science.[73] Breaking off what had begun was therefore out of the question; it must, instead, be continued courageously. And in the subsequent period, the results achieved repeatedly attracted public recognition: in the fields of clinical medicine, education, curative education, and agriculture, and also in art. In 1937 the Goetheanum stage group represented Switzerland at the Paris World Fair with great success, with a performance of a play by Albert Steffen, eurythmy performances, and scenes from Goethe's *Faust*: "Rien de plus intéressant que cette representation à nul autre pareil. Rien de plus émouvant que l'organisation intérieure de ce groupement qu'anime une foi artistique."[74]

*

Thus the section leaders and the communities connected with them became active and productive after Rudolf Steiner's death. The executive council of the General Anthroposophical Society, however, mostly fell apart. The dissonances between individual executive council members had already been present beneath the surface while Rudolf Steiner was alive; soon after his death, disputes and discords without end began. In 1935, after the ground had been prepared through the fomenting of discontent, Ita Wegman and Elisabeth Vreede were expelled from the executive council by a general majority, and were also obliged to give up their section activities. At the same general meeting, almost 2,000 Society members were expelled. This was at a time, two years after Hitler had seized power in Germany, when the united resistance of the Anthroposophical Society would have been more important than ever to the fascist "love of evil" and the "powers of evil" that had taken "grave possession of humanity" (Steiner[75]), along with the impending euthanasia policies, the persecution of anyone who thought differently, and genocide.

The breakdown in the organizational structures initiated by Steiner that occurred (or was completed) in Dornach in 1935, and the final destruction of the "esoteric executive council" formed by him, had many repercussions and left a deep wound in the Society to whose destiny Rudolf Steiner had bound himself. At the same time, this breakdown also injured the School for Spiritual Science.

In Arlesheim, without connection to the Goetheanum, Ita Wegman continued her professional work in the fields of medicine, curative education, and social work. Without a doubt her work had been the most impressive and dynamic impulse of the School for reaching out into the non-anthroposophic public domain. But now, all the clinical-therapeutic and pharmaceutical research work in Arlesheim, including mistletoe production, thus lost their connection with the Dornach School. The Goetheanum retained the patents to remedies that Rudolf Steiner had once developed in collaboration with Oskar Schmiedel and Ita Wegman, along with its shares in Weleda. This fact, however, did not prevent anyone from noticing that the field of scientific and pharmaceutical (and also therapeutic art) research and development; and the whole domain of medical and curative education training and activity, had come adrift from the School; so that the Dornach hill was increasingly impoverished, and indeed, was sidelining itself. Rudolf Steiner had looked forward to the construction of a School clinic at the Goetheanum. Instead, Ita Wegman was called the "carcinoma of the Anthroposophical Society" after his death[76] ("my dear friend and colleague in the medical field and also other areas of spiritual-scientific research");[77] and ultimately everything connected with her was removed from Dornach. Elisabeth Vreede also continued working in Arlesheim after being dismissed, tirelessly devoting herself to her fields of mathematics and astronomy, extended by spiritual science. The loss of the observatory she had built up at the Goetheanum, and the disbanding of her section periodicals and the "Rudolf Steiner Archive at the Goetheanum" after her expulsion had many consequences, and damaged the core of her work. In Stuttgart, the faculty of teachers at the Waldorf School also fell into the disputes and conflicts raging in the Anthroposophical Society. Highly gifted, innovative teachers (including Eugen Kolisko, Caroline von Heydebrand, and Herbert Hahn), upon whom Rudolf Steiner had relied for academic rigor, left the school. The Pedagogical Section at the Goetheanum, which for Rudolf Steiner was one of the most important, along with the sections for medicine, science, and art, simply withered until it lost all significance. From then on the work of the Waldorf School continued without any real connection to the Goetheanum, which no longer had any capacity to offer educational impetus, guidance, or creativity. Even Marie Steiner finally left the place, going into exile after grave quarrels with Albert Steffen and Guenther Wachsmuth. What remained was the large and mainly empty building of a Society that had collapsed into itself.

*

Because of these catastrophic developments, despite the individual section work that began in 1924 and continued after March 30, 1925, the General Anthroposophical Society and the Dornach Goetheanum never became the "reality" of which Rudolf Steiner had spoken at the Christmas Foundation Meeting. Split into factions, and for the most part without anyone taking over the "tasks" for which "people outside can have respect," the Society played no noteworthy role in the wider conflicts and debates that unfolded in the world during the following decades, or in fact throughout the twentieth century. Nor did the Goetheanum, as the School for Spiritual Science and head-quarters of the General Anthroposophical Society, ever come to exert an active influence on public life in the sense envisioned by Rudolf Steiner. The innovative research results in the fields of agriculture and medicine that Steiner described on December 31, 1923, as being necessary for making a sustained impression in the public domain, and which were to prepare a real paradigm shift, were never published, or even compiled, by the School for Spiritual Science.

Scientific research work did not entirely cease, however, and those working in the Glass House always retained a strong awareness of their tasks and responsibility. In the decades after Steiner's death, nevertheless, almost all preconditions were lacking for the great breakthrough he had hoped could happen. The social community of highly gifted, even brilliant individuals had been fractured and destroyed, taking down a great deal with it. Especially in the time after Rudolf Steiner's death, mutually cooperating forces of all the scientists, physicians, and artists working in Dornach would have been needed to be able to find "the most precise scientific methods and guidelines" out of anthroposophy, without their spiritual teacher. This would have been a form of collaboration and mutual enhancement in which people, as professional *and* esoteric community, could grow beyond themselves into the spiritual dimension of the School. In the first years after Rudolf Steiner's death, the Glass House at the Goetheanum was still such a place—where young scientists, motivated and inspired by Steiner, shared their work and met each other. They included gifted and innovative researchers such as Ehrenfried Pfeiffer and Rudolf Hauschka. But then these scientists, too, who had previously been in close professional connection, were drawn into different camps of the conflict and broke off almost all communication with each other, so that common work became inconceivable. The singularly capable researcher Lilly Kolisko, whose work Rudolf Steiner had repeatedly praised in the highest terms, also became a victim of the Society's destruction and ended her days in exile in England, impoverished and alone. Others also left, never to return. "The aim of the Anthroposophical Society will be to promote and support spiritual research, and that of the School for Spiritual Science to engage in this research itself..."

Given these developments, the continuation of the concept of the "School for Spiritual Science," along with the unbroken tradition since 1923/24 of the Goetheanum's claim to lead the General Anthroposophical Society; and likewise the Christmas Foundation Meeting as a reference basis, became increasingly questionable and problematic. However, no discussion of fundamental principles was initiated at the Goetheanum. People became increasingly distanced from reality, living with lofty concepts they could no longer measure up to, but which, nevertheless, remained in use, and were seemingly legitimized. Back in 1923, Rudolf Steiner had already warned against using nomenclatures without doing them justice. ("The second thing is that this Goetheanum has the supplementary title of "School for Spiritual Science," invoking the supposition of demonstrating scientific achievements. However extensive our opponents, they must not be able to find fault. It is impossible to counter this opposition with the edifice of a Goetheanum, of this School for Spiritual Science, if it can be shown that nothing scientific is accomplished there."[78])

*

After the end of the Second World War, people started coming to Dornach again, including many young people who had been on the front lines, and in whom there now lived an existential mood of hopeful new beginnings and dawning horizons. The Waldorf schools in Germany started their work anew, and received much encouragement from the general public. Many other anthroposophic activities likewise experienced resurgence, following cultural catastrophe and the now-apparent spiritual crisis. Yet the Goetheanum had been irrevocably harmed by the shocks and ruptures in the Society and the School, which led to the sundering of the executive council and section collegium. The events that had occurred, and their far-reaching consequences for the Society and the School for Spiritual Science, were never properly worked through. No inquiry was undertaken into the destructive processes, and the people and institutions affected by this were not rehabilitated; nor was there any discussion about the impact of the loss that the School (and thus the scientific work) had suffered in consequence. What did occur, on the other hand, was an honest attempt by executive council members and section colleagues who had remained in Dornach to reunite people in Society and professional work. Meetings and conferences took place at which professional findings were exchanged, and anthroposophic lectures were held. Fundamental work on spiritual-scientific perspectives in each professional field was restarted, and many young people gained impulses for the future at Goetheanum meetings, the former locus of Rudolf Steiner's activity, through real, intergenerational connections. The Goetheanum was, however, still far removed (more so than ever, in fact) from what Steiner had aspired to as a serious school for spiritual science undertaking research, teaching, publication, and training. If the School as intended by Steiner had been able to unite its forces with the General Anthroposophical Society; and if, after offering common, concerted spiritual resistance, they had survived German fascism and the Second World War; there is much to suggest that immediately after 1945 they would have become a significant influence in the science and culture of Central Europe during the following years of general turbulence, attempts at "de-Nazification," and spiritual reorientation.

Instead of this, because of its internal disintegration, the Anthroposophical Society turned back in upon itself, and was once again (or still) preoccupied with its own dire condition. Soon after the war, very vibrant "School weeks" were held in

Stuttgart at the Waldorf School; yet in the years after 1945, the Society did not succeed in becoming the active organ of anthroposophy's cultural influence that Rudolf Steiner had so urgently demanded in 1923/24. In many places, distance from Dornach was maintained for a long time because it was seen as the seat of all the crises. It was rightly regarded not as a center of scientific activity, but of anthroposophic art, which had survived the war and continued to develop. Likewise, the separation between the Clinical-Therapeutic Institute in Arlesheim and the Goetheanum remained in place. The clinic continued its work in accordance with Ita Wegman's ideas, cultivating international relationships with patients and therapists. Both Ita Wegman and Elisabeth Vreede had died in 1943, five years before Marie Steiner (1948). Albert Steffen and Guenther Wachsmuth continued to manage the Goetheanum, and (in their own way) the Anthroposophical Society. Almost nothing remained of what had been started there in 1923/24; and even the work of the Estate Association, founded by Marie Steiner to publish Rudolf Steiner's lectures and writings, was undertaken outside the auspices of the Goetheanum and the so-called "School," in mutual enmity. For a long time, the volumes of the developing Complete Works (GAs) were prohibited from sale at the Goetheanum. Statements Rudolf Steiner had made in 1923/24 about the task of the School and the sections were unpublished for a long time, and unknown to most members. The configuration of the place as he intended it, did not live in their awareness; or increasingly faded from it, until it lapsed into the forgotten.

Nevertheless, the sections continued to be developed to a modest extent after the war, with great personal commitment from all the participants, and on a more or less voluntary basis. The sections had a social focus, trying to connect people and keep them together in their professional work. The esoteric lessons of the First Class continued to take place, based on word-for-word stenographic transcripts. During the further course of the twentieth century, increasing numbers of people contributed at professional conferences in Dornach their own anthroposophic studies and research, which they had undertaken elsewhere. Rudolf Steiner had intended the Goetheanum to be a perceptive organ for anthroposophic work throughout the world—a center to which anthroposophists could gratefully report on the results of their work. This dynamic now occurred with increasing intensity, at the invitation of the Goetheanum executive council and/ or the section leader. This activity offered real support and aid to a place that had almost entirely lost the qualities of a "center," and basically was being kept alive only by the "periphery." Against the background of the given reality, that is, the reality created through destruction; the Dornach sections (and the entire School for Spiritual Science) defined themselves in consequence, ever more clearly as organs of communication and coordination; of perception, and "networking" of activities that occurred elsewhere. The Goetheanum became a major forum of meeting; a place to reflect international anthroposophic endeavors. This aspect of the Goetheanum and School had been a major part of Rudolf Steiner's concept from the beginning; but as a sole, dominant aspect, it was in fact a considerable abbreviation and distortion of what had originally been intended for Dornach. Rudolf Steiner had always understood the Goetheanum as being *also* an organ of perception, but embedded in the overall context of observation *and* dynamic movement, perception *and* impetus. He had described the Goetheanum as the heart-organ of the General Anthroposophical Society and its School; and never allowed any doubt that what had been founded at Dornach, and its designation as *School*, would be justified only insofar as the Goetheanum contributed to the scientific, artistic, and social challenges of the present through its *own* research work, publications, and actions. It was for this reason that Rudolf Steiner worked so very closely with his colleagues and discussed far-reaching plans—including, right up to the last moment, the potential building of a new anthroposophic clinic on the Dornach hill: a center of healing alongside a center of knowledge. As outlined briefly above, he sought the development of an anthroposophic center at the Goetheanum with comprehensive research activities, methodical and diverse training courses, and practice-oriented institutions, where the results of research could be directly realized. The compost preparations, for instance, that Steiner described to the farmers at Koberwitz, had been tried out previously at his direction, by Ehrenfried Pfeiffer and Guenther Wachsmuth in Dornach. Steiner comprehensively applied this procedure in the whole field of anthroposophic medicine and pharmacy, and also of anthroposophic art.

But despite the new beginnings and the intensifying section activities in the second half of the twentieth century, the Goetheanum was still a long way from this goal. Decisive connections had been ruptured, and important individuals had departed. There was little or nothing to be seen of the desired "center of importance" for the world as a leading contributor to Central European cultural and spiritual life, or of the possibility to create these developments. The tragedy of the twentieth century had taken its toll (the "time of great decisions"), both on the outside world as well as inside the Society that Rudolf Steiner had re-founded in 1923/24. The Medical Section in particular, however, tried in the second half of the twentieth century to make the best of the actual situation; though it was a situation that was no longer easy to change. Over the decades the Section gathered together people working in therapeutic fields throughout the world to further the common goal. It tried to overcome divisions, to support mutual perception and work, and to cultivate a connection with the spiritual content of Rudolf Steiner's life's work, and that of Ita Wegman. One of the most far-reaching proposals for a reform of the Dornach School and the configuration of its sections; with the aim of responding properly to the actual situation in Dornach and in the world, was made—not by chance—by a physician, clinic and university founder Gerhard Kienle in 1976. He would have been very glad also to participate in such a reform in person, but this did not come about.

*

How Rudolf Steiner would judge the communal structure that today exists at the Goetheanum is, naturally, hard to say. With the growth of internationally active professional groups and improved global communications, the social tasks of the Dornach sections have grown enormously, not only at times of big conferences, but also in general. The sections serve the anthroposophical work that is undertaken internationally in their professional field. In relation to this decidedly *social* orientation, Rudolf Steiner gave exemplary praise to Elisabeth Vreede's section work in mathematics and astronomy. [79] As a big, international conference center, the Goetheanum still offers the unique opportunity, which is available nowhere else in the world, for people who work in a professional field to meet there, to engage in further training and to connect more deeply with the Being of anthroposophy, or with Dornach's true cultural concerns. This significance of the Goetheanum as a place that "leads human souls throughout the world together to collaborate in harmony" was something Rudolf Steiner stressed from the beginning,[80] no doubt foreseeing that the need for and possibility of such encounter and collaboration would continue to grow in the twentieth century (and beyond).

On the other hand, the question remains in relation to Rudolf Steiner's concept of the Dornach School, as to how the sections can really "resolve" the "scientific and artistic tasks" assigned to them, which their founder spoke of equally. As long as one does not impose a distorted interpretation on it, or extend it beyond its actual scope (which would be more or less tantamount to annulling it) the concept of the sections, collegium and School is still founded upon profession-specific research, teaching, publication and training *on-site*. And all people who work at the Goetheanum know that many of these activities scarcely exist in Dornach; and because of the economic situation, are tending to diminish still further. In addition, only a few of the former (artistic) study and training opportunities at and around the

Goetheanum remain; and the research and publication capacities of the sections are more than restricted, for reasons both of staffing and funding, not to mention an inadequate level of individual capacities. Who can dispute that the kind of research desired and envisioned by Rudolf Steiner requires special, even singular, talents and gifts? But after March 30, 1925, the development of the General Anthroposophical Society and the Goetheanum by no means drew brilliant individuals toward it; and, if it had, the on-site working facilities would have been very poor for them. Productive and critical discourse with leading academics and researchers as desired by Steiner (with people working in their fields at the limits of knowledge and understanding) is now something done elsewhere, at least in its germinal form. To reverse this trend and return Dornach to its original task would require infrastructure, and professional and staff conditions, for which there is next to no foundation at the Goetheanum. Irrespective of this, the (almost still greater) difficulty exists that the concept of the sections used by Rudolf Steiner implies, as previously suggested, a well-developed spiritual or esoteric level: ultimately, true spiritual research, as this occurred during Steiner's lifetime in collaboration with the leader of the School. The question as to how, without Rudolf Steiner, *spiritual-scientific* specialist research can be pursued in Dornach, thus realizing his concept of the sections and the School, has scarcely been openly discussed since 1925. Failing to discuss this problem, or overlooking it through audacious assumptions, will by no means lead us further. The life work of the researcher and initiate Rudolf Steiner was a unique event in the twentieth century.

Against this background, the question remains as to whether it might not be an urgent necessity, and a more honest approach, to distance oneself clearly from Rudolf Steiner's former development plans and aims for the School; instead, updating and reformulating Dornach's current and future task in a way commensurate with actual circumstances. This redefinition of the center would have to arise from a sober appraisal and human modesty.

Among other things, it would have to ask which sections today still have a real, professional justification for their work (that is, are really *needed*), and how they might be able to define and, in the best way possible, fulfill their tasks as coordination organs of international professional work, in the sense of a secretariat that makes no claim to spiritual-scientific research or (both exoteric and esoteric) leadership. Gerhard Kienle's proposal in 1976, by contrast, envisioned retaining a certain leadership role, but one where the section leaders (in a *collegiate* context) are in future no longer present in Dornach themselves, but instead continue with their professional tasks in the world. In other words, they would direct anthroposophic institutions or undertake academic tasks at universities. In relation to the Medical Section, Kienle wrote, among other things:

> Individuals who are section leaders must be able to represent the medical movement both internally and publicly. They must, however, also distinguish themselves through actual accomplishments. They must be able to assess which physicians bring to expression a spiritual leadership of the medical movement. In other words, they must note the achievements and productivity of individuals, and be able to evaluate and acknowledge this. Furthermore, they must at least be able to approximately judge the significance of specialist medical issues for humanity; to grasp overall contexts, and to plan and implement long-term projects. They must also not only be able to initiate their own spiritual work, but also to integrate that of others in an overall framework, and bring it to fruition. They must not shy away from making and taking responsibility for decisions of major scope and importance. The section leadership would set its own rules of procedure. There is no need for it to be based in Dornach. It is conceivable that tasks can be distributed (that is, responsibility for work in diverse countries). The section leaders could have assistants who

also work on their behalf. The section leader should be supported by a section manager based in Dornach, whose task involves communicating; organizing and coordinating conferences, meetings, and so forth.[82]

It is not known whether this proposal by Gerhard Kienle, which he sent to Dornach, was ever discussed at the Goetheanum. If it had been implemented, this would have amounted to a major change in the Dornach view of the School. According to Kienle, section leaders should in future be professionals in their field who work in it, in the world, in a position of responsibility and who, from the perspective of their work, have an overview of the whole profession and can lead it in a real sense. A "School" section understood in this sense would describe an already existing international context of work; and the section's capability and performance would equate with what is realized in the world for each anthroposophic professional discipline, in optimum coordination and collaboration. Without doubt Kienle, who had a realistic and sober way of appraising situations, largely took proper account of actual circumstances. The section secretaries were to be based in Dornach to coordinate activities and prepare gatherings which, when they reached a certain size, could, or would have to, take place at the Goetheanum. Dornach would be the suitable place for *that*; but realistically, from a professional perspective, it was in fact nothing more than a space for conferences.

*

Gerhard Kienle thus suggested a possible way forward for anthroposophic professional domains ("sections") that had *living potential* (i.e. those that undertook work in the world and were needed by it). If one rejects such a procedure because of an existential concern to preserve Rudolf Steiner's original concept of the School, or to achieve it once again, one must ask what could be done at the Goetheanum now and in the future, to still eventually give full reality to what Steiner envisioned. In the context of the sections, it seems worth noting, among other things, that Rudolf Steiner (as emphasized previously) envisioned not only the development of an anthroposophic clinic as "model institution"[83] *at the Goetheanum*, but also the founding of other facilities that would demonstrate the efficacy of the specialist sections, and that were at the same time to be centers of research and training. Steiner's opportunities to do this were extremely limited at the beginning of the twentieth century; even continuing the little "Friedwart" Waldorf School on the Dornach hill was forbidden to him by the authorities. Nevertheless, there is much to suggest that Rudolf Steiner wished wherever possible to set up "active centers" *at the Goetheanum* for all specialist sections of the School (not just for medicine); that is, institutions where work could be done and demonstrated. A "model school" at or close to the Goetheanum, with a highly qualified anthroposophic faculty of teachers and motivated parents could, in collaboration with the Pedagogical Section (that is, with help from the section leader and subject to his responsibility) could demonstrate, in proximity to the Goetheanum, the real capability of anthroposophic pedagogy when practiced at a high level. Such a model, realized in all Sections, accorded with Steiner's ideas. Out in the world, anthroposophy must often work under difficult circumstances, adapting to meager conditions and just doing whatever is possible with them, in the realms of medicine, education, curative education, and social work. Thus many compromises with actual realities are necessary. To maintain a Waldorf school in a socially disadvantaged inner-city district, with only a few anthroposophically-oriented teachers and next to no corresponding parental homes, is not only hard; its results, too, will be unlikely to offer testimony of the potential capacity and performance of anthroposophic pedagogy. Rudolf Steiner would no doubt nevertheless be in favor of making every effort in the world as it exists. But demonstrating in *exemplary fashion* at the Goetheanum (or in close proximity to it) what spiritual-scientific methodology can achieve in various professional domains through its "ideal model institutions," could be a directly helpful, and by no means elitist, option. The School's social task would consist here in conveying qualitative guidance to the anthroposophic movement and at the same time demonstrating to the public the potential power of anthroposophic methodology in professional fields, when given the conditions it needs to thrive. By contrast, defending anthroposophy publicly while further weakening it internally (or standing by as the "active centers" of former work successively lose their qualitative standards), leads to situations of increasing untruthfulness that are of no service to anthroposophic spiritual science, the work of Rudolf Steiner, and the future of humanity. The founding of model institutions at the Goetheanum, co-run and maintained by Section leaders who play an active part in them, and drawing on the work and commitment of outstanding professionals in the anthroposophic movement, could be a helpful way forward in this situation, and one appropriate to the School. It would help to imbue the School with reality, because the section leaders would continue to work in their professional fields; thus detailed, grounded activities of knowledge development and research would occur in Dornach. Such activity would have a socially configuring character, and would in addition facilitate training or further training options as Rudolf Steiner originally intended. Regard would grow for a Goetheanum surrounded in this way by capable, responsibly-led School institutions offering training and advanced training, and this would very likely also influence potential funders and donors.

For the artistic sections, on the other hand, such a concept would make the Goetheanum itself—as total artwork—the primary locus of demonstrable value. In the future, the profile of Dornach would be informed not by brought-in productions, but by what would be shown on the stage under the *section's auspices and responsibility*. Such productions, in other words, would have been devised at the Goetheanum. In Marie Steiner's day, this responsibility was personalized and successfully exercised. Under her direction there was high regard for the Goetheanum stage. She bore sole responsibility for her work, creating its influential style through her inner connection with Rudolf Steiner and the foundations of anthroposophy. From the Goetheanum, troupes of actors and eurythmists went on tour, eventually returning again, and kindled worldwide interest in the distinctive artistic work done at Dornach. Over and above this, the Goetheanum itself is also a world-class architectural work. Ensuring its preservation and working further on its interior forms, or filling its space with substance, is among the primary responsibilities of the corresponding School section. The order of the day (and of the future) is not to "modernize" and adapt the Goetheanum to the purpose-built structures of modernity, but to configure the place increasingly as a "mystery center": an edifice which gives us the experience, as we cross its threshold, that more is involved here than the ordinary business of daily life.

Active work on these *professional* tasks at the Goetheanum, and very probably *only* this work, bears within it the possibility of once again approaching the productive sources of anthroposophy in Dornach, and thus also of Rudolf Steiner's own individuality. As the real accomplishment of work and knowledge, in creative engagement with specific tasks, it would facilitate an esotericism of action, which distinguished Rudolf Steiner's life work and the development of the anthroposophic movement; and which can never be present (solely) in the management of coordinating, administrative or rhetorical tasks. *"The gods descend to us in our deeds"* (Ita Wegman). If such a path were pursued intentionally and with united forces, this would by no means inevitably ensure an esoteric connection with Rudolf Steiner. There is much to suggest, however, that accomplishing work in this way might develop the perspective of such closeness; a connection that once again brings to expression the spiritual dimension of section work and community, and would thus form the basis for all further development. As we saw before, Rudolf Steiner relied on this continuing endeavor in inner connection with his work and individuality. The words of Christ, "Where two or three are gathered together in my name, there I am in the midst of them" (Matthew 18:20) do not apply only to the esoteric community of the first Christians.

*

The position of the current Dornach executive council within the School for Spiritual Science, highlighted as problematic in a key passage in the annual general meeting motion, intrinsically throws up many developmental questions beyond those of staffing. There is no doubt that all the executive council members in 1923/24 at the same time bore responsibility for sections (though by contrast, no later[84] than Maria Röschl's appointment as leader of the Youth Section, not all section leaders were members of the executive council). In the way outlined earlier, and elsewhere more precisely detailed, the executive council members had special working relationships with Rudolf Steiner, and were individuals who had achieved high regard in their profession, and to some extent at least, a position in the world. ("In the world, a great deal does after all depend on the fact that there are individuals working within anthroposophy who are otherwise engaged in life."[85]) They did not work fulltime on the executive council but continued to work in their professional fields: ItaWegman in the clinic, Marie Steiner on the stage, Albert Steffen with his literary works and the newsletter, Elisabeth Vreede in the Rudolf Steiner Archive and (later) at the observatory, Guenther Wachsmuth on the Goetheanum building.

The executive council positions after 1923/24 acquired an extraordinarily high standing among members of the Anthroposophical Society because of the significance that Rudolf

Steiner assigned to the esoteric executive council (Urvorstand) at the Goetheanum and the School for Spiritual Science; and also because of the individuals who formed the original executive council (Urvorstand), whose destinies were connected with Rudolf Steiner. Not only their luster, but also the scope of their power (which executive roles within the Theosophical and Anthroposophical Societies did not have at all prior to 1923/24), derived exclusively from the Christmas Foundation Meeting, at which Rudolf Steiner designated the executive council appointed by him as the "locus of full authority";[86] although this was *solely* in the context of the *overall concept* of the Society and School that he developed and highlighted with such insistence. Rudolf Steiner was absolutely aware of the problem of "curule chairs" in the leadership echelons of the Anthroposophical Society,[87] and there is little to suggest that in the internal design of the Goetheanum he would have assigned anything like the spatial dimensions of the executive council rooms that they were later given. Steiner knew how easily seduced and vain many people within the Anthroposophical Society are, both members and office-holders; he also knew how a place like Dornach can potentially become associated with blindness and bedazzlement; with loss of reality, in fact; and he spoke of "School preciousness" and "other airs and graces."[88] Nevertheless, he trusted the people he had appointed, and considered them capable of properly representing anthroposophy (also after his death) both *to the world* and *in the world*:

> There is a difference between promoting, in a sectarian fashion, something one has taken possession of as dogmatic anthroposophy; and honest, open, unconcealed and unvarnished support of knowledge of the spiritual world arising through anthroposophy in a way that enables people to gain a dignified relationship to this world. The task of the executive council at the Goetheanum is to take up work for anthroposophy in the latter way alone.[89]

Rudolf Steiner repeatedly stressed that, after the Christmas Foundation Meeting, the executive council at the Goetheanum would never again, as previously, be an "administrative executive" preoccupied chiefly with the Anthroposophical Society, its members, conferences and problems. In marked distinction to this, its task as *initiative* executive council was outlined by Rudolf Steiner with great emphasis, and this creative responsibility extended through to the specialist fields. Rudolf Steiner was no longer present at the separation of the office of executive council members from responsibility for specialist fields, which developed decades later, with the danger of an ultimately disengaged form of "representation" or sole focus on the Society. This separation certainly did not, and does not, accord with the Christmas Foundation Meeting. It was introduced at a time, however, when many other, sustaining elements of the Christmas Foundation Meeting were no longer alive in Dornach; and core figures of destiny were lacking, without whom Rudolf Steiner also would not have proceeded in the way he did. The connection of the office of executive council member with that of section leader made immediate sense within his School concept. However, it also depended on the presence of people who were capable of working for the Goetheanum, anthroposophic spiritual science, for Rudolf Steiner and the Society; and *at the same time* of accomplishing high-quality work in their own fields of expertise, as well as leading a professional section community in a social sense.

There is likewise no doubt that in post-war developments and increasing internationalization of relationships, the extent of the section leaders' tasks grew along with their coordinating, structural, and administrative duties. As a social entity, the Anthroposophical Society did not become more straightforward. Bringing the sections up to the standard appropriate for them within Rudolf Steiner's School concept (as spiritually-founded faculties of the esoteric School, working scientifically and socially, where relevant, running "model institutes," and offering training) was increasingly seen as a distinct lifework; and indeed, as the task of a collegiate community far too great for a single person, *insofar* as this whole scope of section activity (or Steiner's concept of the section) is actually seen and intended. It was also perceived ever more clearly that the luciferic danger of the "cult of the personality" and of focus on individuals, and thus also of potential exercise of power, does not exist only at the executive council level, since section leaders can potentially assert both an exoteric and esoteric leadership claim.

For executive council members without section responsibility, however, the theoretical question arose and still arises as to what their *intrinsic* tasks are within the Goetheanum concept—tasks which "the public can respect." The organization of conferences for members, or even of meetings and sessions with other Society officials, are certainly not adequate as a job description within Rudolf Steiner's School concept, even if they can be undertaken in a way that demands much time and energy. In the near future, too, it will no longer be possible to finance them. As we saw previously, Rudolf Steiner wanted a School that works into the world and instigates major cultural impulses, not one that largely just meets itself. The Anthroposophical Society is an organ or an instrument for enabling anthroposophy to become effective in the world. Inasmuch as it fulfils this task, it is purposeful and justified. As a Society, it has the function of serving, and should help people to find anthroposophy:

> Today we live at a time when, basically, anthroposophy ought to become a burning question for countless people on earth, if the Anthroposophical Society only succeeded in really working in a way that enables people to be set alight by their need of what comes to meet them in anthroposophy.[90]

Rudolf Steiner saw the issues thus summarized as a priority task of the executive council at the Goetheanum. It is a task which seems to have lost none of its relevance. Steiner relied on the initiating work of the executive council in the General Anthroposophical Society and in the world, undertaken with a high level of expertise and in the direct way outlined. Insofar as the office of executive council member at the Goetheanum is realized, the tasks and responsibilities involved surely include representing Rudolf Steiner's core anthroposophy at a high level, and encouraging members of the Anthroposophical Society to do the same. Connected with this, is real protection for the being and work of Rudolf Steiner. Failing to emphatically oppose grave defamations and intentional lies that gain wide circulation (as in publications by Helmut Zander) is wholly irreconcilable, as Steiner would view it, with holding a responsible position at the Goetheanum, and is not even acceptable for members of the First Class. "Representing" the Goetheanum executive council to members of the Anthroposophical Society is not necessary, since members know the people concerned.

In contrast, Rudolf Steiner's idea of representation related essentially to the non-anthroposophic, public domain. It was there that real anthroposophy and the spiritual concerns of the Goetheanum and the School for Spiritual Science were to become visible through executive council members, specifically and in proactive ways through their professional expertise, their anthroposophic knowledge and capacity. In addition the executive council's tasks included, and still include, working to ensure that the Goetheanum does actually become an international center of anthroposophic spiritual science; a "competency center" in the modern use of the word, which can be internally strong and exert effective influence. In this sense, the task areas of the executive council at the Goetheanum include developing the General Anthroposophical Section. This would offer a base for competently acknowledging the extensive work and essential being of Rudolf Steiner, with the aid of important publications and editions related to his biography and oeuvre that ought to be produced and disseminated by the

Goetheanum. Over and above this, core contributions from the General Anthroposophical Section or from the executive council members at all specialist conferences at the Goetheanum are of great importance. This is because it will in future be essential for those working in specialist fields not to lose their connection to the core of anthroposophy (as a living "being") in the challenges of their daily work. At present and in future much depends on whether Waldorf schools and other "anthroposophic" institutions really succeed in keeping their spiritual foundations alive, or in grasping them anew, in difficult circumstances; or whether they will continue to succumb to disengaged standardization, in which co-worker groups have only a small, somewhat besieged minority of people committed to anthroposophy. In 1923/24, Rudolf Steiner urged the Anthroposophical Society—and the executive council at the Goetheanum—to take on *responsibility*, finally, for the founding of anthroposophic institutions in the world. Further elaboration of the Anthroposophical Society in this direction (instead of relativization of anthroposophy) lies in the obligations and responsibilities of a Goetheanum leadership insofar as it wishes to still take its lead from Rudolf Steiner, or to be connected with him, and also lies within the task area of the General Anthroposophical Society itself. According to Steiner, the Dornach School should "spiritualize" the Anthroposophical Society through its professional and esoteric work; this Society itself—or its membership—should however view the flourishing of anthroposophic institutions as a matter of its own concern. Rudolf Steiner did not expect of future members an endless flow of letters to executive council members about problems and contentious individuals within the Anthroposophical Society, nor numerous discussions, meetings of those who hold responsibilities, conferences, and multi-colored prospectuses, but instead a shared responsibility for realizing the path of anthroposophy in the world.

*

Whether the Goetheanum as the School for Spiritual Science can really go forward into the future, and arrive there, is currently very questionable certainly, not just for financial reasons. The importance of the Goetheanum could, however, be very great in the future; here—and *only* here—thousands of physicians, therapists, nurses, teachers, curative educators, social workers, farmers and artists in the anthroposophical movement gather each year, in efforts to sustain modern spiritual science, and perspectives and concerns in the world that are related to it. Often they do so under difficult and impoverished conditions. If it proves possible in the future to turn the Goetheanum once more into a locus of concentration, encounter, and strengthening—rather than a modern, multipurpose events hall (with advertising space)—this would be an important step forward. From the Goetheanum, and with the help of the General Anthroposophical Society, a new culture of anthroposophic spiritual-scientific study and research could emerge into the present and future; influencing anthroposophic institutions and helping to rebuild seminars and training courses in various places; and could fill them with new, intense life. There is a rich spiritual legacy in Rudolf Steiner's lectures and writings, which has so far been tapped, and applied in our culture, to a limited extent only. Many perspectives and new developments contained there for a new medicine, education, curative education, and agriculture, as well as for social, religious and artistic life, possess a significance whose relevance in our current cultural crisis and in many of its practical domains is becoming ever more apparent. Despite this, anthroposophic training courses (both general and profession-specific) in which the originating substance of anthroposophy is really studied, have grown ever fewer in number in recent decades, as have anthroposophic bookstores and diverse institutions that were once of great importance. Rather than standing by helplessly as this happens, but instead reacting to it responsibly (that is, by making efforts to counter this trend) is something that lies in the area of responsibility of the General Anthroposophical Society and its leadership in Dornach.

"Today we live at a time when, basically, anthroposophy ought to become a burning question for countless people on earth if the Anthroposophical Society only succeeded in really working in a way that enables people to be set alight by their need of what comes to meet them in anthroposophy..."

If this endeavor fails, the Goetheanum will no longer be in the least sustainable in the medium and longer term, nor will its upkeep be financially justifiable. Rudolf Steiner endeavored to create a mystery center on the Dornach hill, but while he was still alive he sometimes had the impression "that all feeling has been lost for what really ought to be given by anthroposophy."[91] Rudolf Steiner did not wish for any kind of self-promotion by "administrators"; nor an interview culture in the weekly periodical *Das Goetheanum*; nor any of the habitual usages of journalism; instead, he sought compelling work that speaks for itself. The fact that Otto Schily, the former German Red Army Faction solicitor and later interior minister, gave a talk at the Goetheanum in which he expressed his thanks for anthroposophy, but also his doubts about the likely errors in Steiner's spiritual research, would very probably have interested the founder of anthroposophy. Together with Albert Steffen, however, Rudolf Steiner would never have been willing to disseminate such an occurrence prominently in the periodical *Das Goetheanum,* while in the same issue just mentioning in passing, in journalistic style, the birthday conference lasting several days that was organized by the Anthroposophical Society in Switzerland (together with the Goetheanum executive council) and that included numerous anthroposophic contributions. Rudolf Steiner asked Albert Steffen to edit *Das Goetheanum* to a high standard, and really to publish anthroposophic articles in it—that is, with original spiritual-scientific content.[92] Likewise, Steiner established the newsletter in order to have the impulse or the "will" of the Christmas Foundation Meeting present within it.[93]

Throughout his life, Rudolf Steiner took a keen interest in the world, its problems and concerns, developments, dangers and opportunities. There is no doubt that he placed the Goetheanum *into the world*; but at the same time he never permitted the slightest doubt that the existence of this building and center is justified only if it is capable of elaborating and demonstrating its own, new anthroposophic achievements. Ultimately he hoped that such *achievements* would be acknowledged; but not by merely external acknowledgement to satisfy personal vanity.

To conclude and summarize, Rudolf Steiner relied on work and human modesty as the essentials of a real future for the Goetheanum. He repeatedly spoke of the need to overcome all "cult of personalities," and of the "exclusion of absolutely everything of a personal nature."[94] When he sought to establish the "Stiftung für theosophische Art und Kunst" (Foundation for Theosophical Art and Way of Life) in accordance with this principle, Rudolf Steiner stated that the curators should not be invested with "honors" and "dignities" but only with "duties."[95] Steiner described these attributes as the precondition for really acting esoterically; thus certainly also characterizing future circumstances at the Goetheanum.

We can and must question, surely, *whether*, and if feasible *how*, Rudolf Steiner's demanding concept of the School for Spiritual Science can be realized at all without him, as initiate. It does, however, strike one as grave and highly dubious to attempt to perpetuate the institutions he founded, and the names he gave them, without at the same time honoring the obligations and tasks associated with them. Rudolf Steiner was always in favor of flexibility, change, and also humor; anything fixed and dogmatic was alien to him. Since his time, though, little has changed regarding anthroposophy's world tasks and the problems of civilization; and neither, therefore, has the underlying purpose of the School for Spiritual Science altered. To grasp "the flourishing of anthroposophy as a concern of contemporary civilization"[96] remains an undiminished task of the General Anthroposophical Society and of each individual anthroposophist. Rudolf Steiner did not have many colleagues and friends who could work at this level in tangible ways; that is, who not only understood his concerns, but could also personally contribute to their realization. For this it was and is necessary for an individual to be fully anchored in the world; to be imbued by anthroposophy in the deep strata of his being; and to show absolute dedication of will. In addition, progress on the path of inner schooling is needed; so that besides overcoming personal vanity, the ever-present temptations of power and domination are left behind. The "battle" for the Goetheanum after Rudolf Steiner's death was, to a not inconsiderable degree, a *question of power*—and remains so to this day. People in anthroposophic circles do not often speak of this dimension of events, yet it is profoundly real. That one can get beyond it, and successfully come to dwell *in the world* in another way, when drawing on the spiritual core of anthroposophy, has been demonstrated by the life and work of significant pupils of Rudolf Steiner in the twentieth century; among the most impressive of whom, perhaps, is Dr. Willem Zeylmans van Emmichoven, the General Secretary of the Dutch Anthroposophical Society.[97]

Opportunities for developing the School for Spiritual Science in Dornach, in the way intended by Steiner, are certainly not great at present. This assessment can be disputed only by those who have not really engaged with the full scope of Rudolf Steiner's intentions and goals for such a School; instead, taking from Steiner's lectures and writings only what, in this regard, they feel they can affirm, cope with, and assimilate. The tasks formulated by Rudolf Steiner, particularly also for the specialist sections, are of outstanding significance and can only begin to be fulfilled through gradual, progressive initiation, and many helpful social circumstances. There is only an extremely small number of people who have the necessary prerequisites, capacities, and strength, and who are currently preoccupied with the core concerns of Rudolf Steiner's work; in Central Europe, at least, there are far fewer such people than during Rudolf Steiner's lifetime. As we have already stressed, though, his concept of the School (or at least of the specific sections)

was something he developed in response to capable individuals in his closest circle. Without their presence he would have
relinquished this. He would never have contemplated devising
general programs without any chance of actually realizing them
with actual people. Along with the current dwindling economic
base, all this leaves one feeling skeptical, to put it mildly.

On the other hand, we can definitely hold fast to the thought
that, in its specific concept and intention, Rudolf Steiner established
the School for Spiritual Science for the future; or in other words for
the period after March 30, 1925. He once said in Dornach:

> [...] I believe that it is a good, a healing feeling, if we carry
> forward through all our work the sense of not being up to
> it. Only in this way will we achieve what we might call the
> most possible achievement.[98]

To achieve what is "most possible"—in real humility and self-
lessness—and to prepare the future in tangible ways, keeping its
possibilities open, is surely a worthwhile endeavor. Thus we can
also keep possibilities open for unborn souls who, out of their
particular individuality, and with other powers than ours, may
one day be able to continue what has been begun inadequately,
but is still guided by the *originating archetype* of this work. This
"will for the future" must be present at the Goetheanum, if it
wishes to continue to exist and to preserve what Rudolf Steiner
once initiated with far-sighted vision.

> And we cannot really do better for the dissemination, the
> proper presentation of anthroposophy to the world, than
> by becoming ever more aware of the significant impulse
> that anthroposophy should be for the further progress of
> civilization.[99]

In a world fraught with crisis, besieged by natural and cultural
catastrophes, burdened by countless problems, and with little

sense of orientation, the strong presence of an active and influential Goetheanum might yet still, in the future, be a factor of the first order: "the Goetheanum in the midst of the contemporary cultural crisis," as central locus of suprasensory knowledge of the human being and the cosmos. In a letter to members on January 18, 1924, Rudolf Steiner wrote:

> Ways and means must be found to continue what was intended with anthroposophy from the very beginning.[100]

And what was thus intended "from the very beginning" with anthroposophy, the Goetheanum and the School for Spiritual Science, was not a small matter by any means:

> We must be fully aware that endeavors are today needed toward rediscovering the mysteries.
> The Christmas Foundation Meeting was held in this awareness; for there is an urgent need for a center on earth where mysteries can once again be established. As it progresses, the Anthroposophical Society must become the path toward the renewed mysteries.[101]
> And when these things eventually come to be considered in the world in the right way, the task of the Goetheanum will be properly valued through recognition that the task laid upon it was to renew the mysteries.[102]

Rudolf Steiner placed this renewal of the mysteries into the abysmal period of the twentieth century—a time of rising catastrophes in the natural world and civilization, when humanity's capacity for technological annihilation was first perceived and experienced. During this period, and in the face of huge forces of destruction, Rudolf Steiner founded the core of a truly new beginning; a school for spiritual science that was to be an effective counterweight to misguided developments in civilization, and was to prepare a human future on earth. Rudolf Steiner hastened construction of the Goetheanum shortly before the First World War, and in the spirit of the Fifth Gospel. But the school he prepared (like the Fifth Gospel itself) was broad in scope and duration and was conceived for the future. Initiated at the beginning of the twentieth century, it works on in the subterranean will of many people's destinies, both living and dead, including numerous great souls. Michael Bauer wrote as follows to his friend Christian Morgenstern about the laying of the foundation stone of the first Goetheanum:

> Naturally you have heard about the laying of the foundation stone in Dornach. It must surely be one of the most precious occurrences in our lives that it was granted to us—at least in thoughts—to experience the moment when, after two thousand years of privation, a mystery center once more sanctifies the world. And so, when we are born again, hopefully we will find our way to such a center with all the more certainty.[103]

Notes

All German titles of the works of Rudolf Steiner are from the Rudolf Steiner Gesamtausgabe (GA) published by Rudolf Steiner Verlag, Dornach, Switzerland. Information on the equivalent editions in English in the Collected Works of Rudolf Steiner (CW) can be found at www.steinerbooks.org.

1   Rudolf Steiner: *Die Weihnachtstagung zur Begründung der Allgemeinen Anthroposophischen Gesellschaft 1923/24.* (*The Christmas Conference for the Founding of the General Anthroposophical Society 1923/24.* Anthroposophic Press 1990). GA 260. Dornach 1994, p. 52.
2   In: *Das Goetheanum. Wochenschrift für Anthroposophie*, No. 9, 2011, p. 4.
3   Cf. Peter Selg: *Rudolf Steiner und die Freie Hochschule für Geisteswissenschaft. Die Begründung der "Ersten Klasse."* Arlesheim 2008.
4   Cf. Peter Selg: "Die Medizin muss Ernst machen mit dem geistigen Leben." *Rudolf Steiners Hochschulkurse für die jungen Mediziner.* Dornach 2006; also: *Die Briefkorrespondenz der "jungen Mediziner." Eine dokumentarische Studie zur Rezeption von Rudolf Steiners "Jungmediziner"-Kursen.* Dornach 2005; also: *Helene von Grunelius und Rudolf Steiners Kurse für junge Mediziner. Eine biographische Studie.* Dornach 2003.
5   Rudolf Steiner, quoted from Ita Wegman: "Das Krankenlager, die letzten Tage und Stunden Dr. Steiners." In: Ita Wegman: *An die Freunde.* Arlesheim 1986, p. 7.
6   Rudolf Steiner: *Der Goetheanumgedanke inmitten der Kulturkrisis der Gegenwart.* GA 36. Dornach 1961, p. 309.
7   Rudolf Steiner: *Soziale Ideen – Soziale Wirklichkeit – Soziale Praxis.* GA 337a. Dornach 1999, p. 324.

8   Rudolf Steiner: *Die Weltgeschichte in anthroposophischer Beleuchtung.* (*World History and the Mysteries in the Light of Anthroposophy.* Rudolf Steiner Press 1977). GA 233. Dornach 1991, p. 113.

9   Rudolf Steiner: *Anthroposophische Gemeinschaftsbildung.* (*Awakening to Community.* Anthroposophic Press 1974). GA 257. Dornach 1989, p. 10; author's emphasis.

10 Rudolf Steiner: *Der Goetheanumgedanke inmitten der Kulturkrisis der Gegenwart.* GA 36, p. 309.

11 Rudolf Steiner: *Inneres Wesen des Menschen und Leben zwischen Tod und neuer Geburt.* (*The Inner Nature of Man and Our Life between Death and Rebirth.* Rudolf Steiner Press 1994). GA 153. Dornach 1999, p. 15.

12 Rudolf Steiner: *Der Tod als Lebenswandlung.* (*Death as Metamorphosis of Life.* SteinerBooks 2008). GA 182. Dornach 1996, p. 83f.

13 Friedrich Rittelmeyer: *Meine Lebensbegegnung mit Rudolf Steiner.* Stuttgart 1983, p. 128.

14 Rudolf Steiner: *Die Sendung Michaels.* (See *The Archangel Michael: His Mission and Ours.* SteinerBooks 1994). GA 194. Dornach 1994, p. 197.

15 Rudolf Steiner: *Die Konstitution der Allgemeinen Anthroposophischen Gesellschaft und der Freien Hochschule für Geisteswissenschaft.* (*The Foundation Stone / The Life, Nature and Cultivation of Anthroposophy.* Rudolf Steiner Press 1996). GA 260a. Dornach 1987, p. 278.

16 Ibid, p. 105.

17 Cf. Peter Selg: "Das Schicksalsjahr 1923. Rudolf Steiners Weg zur Weihnachtstagung." In: Sergej O. Prokofieff/Peter Selg: *Die Weihnachtstagung und die Begründung der neuen Mysterien.* Arlesheim 2011, p. 11-38.

18 Rudolf Steiner: *Die Weihnachtstagung zur Begründung der Allgemeinen Anthroposophischen Gesellschaft 1923/24.* (*The Christmas Conference.* AP 1990). GA 260, p. 39.

19 Ibid, p. 270.

20 Rudolf Steiner: *Die Konstitution der Allgemeinen Anthroposophischen Gesellschaft und der Freien Hochschule für*

Geisteswissenschaft. (*The Foundation Stone.* RSP 1996). GA
260a, p. 105.

21 Rudolf Steiner: *Anthroposophische Gemeinschaftsbildung.*
(*Awakening to Community.* AP 1974). GA 257, p. 58.

22 Rudolf Steiner: *Die Geschichte und die Bedingungen
der anthroposophischen Bewegung im Verhältnis zur
Anthro-posophischen Gesellschaft.* (*The Anthroposophic
Movement.* Rudolf Steiner Press 1993). GA 258. Dornach
1981, p. 134.

23 Rudolf Steiner: *Die Weihnachtstagung zur Begründung der
Allgemeinen Anthroposophischen Gesellschaft 1923/24.*
(*The Christmas Conference.* AP 1990). GA 260, p. 93f.

24 Ibid, p. 46.

25 Rudolf Steiner: *Die Geschichte und die Bedingungen der
anthroposophischen Bewegung im Verhältnis zur Anthroposophischen Gesellschaft.* (*The Anthroposophic Movement.*
RSP 1993). GA 258, p. 40.

26 Rudolf Steiner: *Die Weihnachtstagung zur Begründung der
Allgemeinen Anthroposophischen Gesellschaft 1923/24.*
(*The Christmas Conference.* AP 1990). GA 260, p. 280.

27 Rudolf Steiner: *Die Geschichte und die Bedingungen der
anthroposophischen Bewegung im Verhältnis zur Anthroposophischen Gesellschaft.* GA 258, p. 141.

28 Rudolf Steiner: *Das Schicksalsjahr 1923 in der Geschichte der
Anthroposophischen Gesellschaft.* GA 259. Dornach 1991, p. 683.

29 Rudolf Steiner: *Die Konstitution der Allgemeinen Anthroposophischen Gesellschaft und der Freien Hochschule für
Geisteswissenschaft.* (*The Foundation Stone.* RSP 1996). GA
260a, p. 190.

30 Ibid, p. 484.

31 Rudolf Steiner: *Das Schicksalsjahr 1923 in der Geschichte
der Anthroposophischen Gesellschaft.* GA 259, p. 531.

32 Ibid, p. 352.

33 Ibid, p. 484.

34 Ibid. Author's emphasis.

35 Rudolf Steiner: *Die Konstitution der Allgemeinen Anthroposophischen Gesellschaft und der Freien Hochschule für*

Geisteswissenschaft. (*The Foundation Stone.* RSP 1996). GA 260a, p. 420.

36   Rudolf Steiner: *Das Schicksalsjahr 1923 in der Geschichte der Anthroposophischen Gesellschaft.* GA 259, p. 495.

37   Ibid, p. 112.

38   Rudolf Steiner: *Die Konstitution der Allgemeinen Anthroposophischen Gesellschaft und der Freien Hochschule für Geisteswissenschaft.* (*The Foundation Stone.* RSP 1996). GA 260a, p. 115.

39   Ibid, p. 116.

40   Ibid, p. 490.

41   Ibid, p. 371.

42   Ibid, p. 248.

43   Ibid.

44   Ibid, p. 142.

45   Rudolf Steiner: *Damit der Mensch ganz Mensch werde.* GA 82. Dornach 1994, p. 246.

46   November 22, 1923. In: Peter Selg: *Dr. Oskar Schmiedel. Der erste anthroposophische Pharmazeut und Weleda-Direktor.* Arlesheim 2010, p. 120.

47   Rudolf Steiner: *Die Weihnachtstagung zur Begründung der Allgemeinen Anthroposophischen Gesellschaft 1923/24.* (*The Christmas Conference.* AP 1990). GA 260, p. 48.

48   Ibid, p. 52.

49   Ibid, p. 222.

50   Rudolf Steiner: *Die Konstitution der Allgemeinen Anthroposophischen Gesellschaft und der Freien Hochschule für Geisteswissenschaft.* (*The Foundation Stone.* RSP 1996). GA 260a, p. 278.

51   Rudolf Steiner: *Das Initiaten-Bewusstsein.* (*True and False Paths in Spiritual Investigation.* Rudolf Steiner Press 1985). GA 243, lectures of August 14 and 21, 1924. Cf. in this respect: Emanuel Zeylmans van Emmichoven: *Wer war Ita Wegman.* Volume 2. Heidelberg 1992, p. 99ff.; as well as Peter Selg: *"Ich bin für Fortschreiten." Ita Wegman und die medizinische Sektion.* Dornach 2002, p. 53f.

52   Rudolf Steiner: *Meditative Betrachtungen und Anleitungen*

zur Vertiefung der Heilkunst. (Course for Young Doctors. Mercury Press 1997). GA 316. Dornach 2003, p. 137. Cf. also Peter Selg: "Die Medizin muss Ernst machen mit dem geistigen Leben." Rudolf Steiners Hochschulkurse für die jungen Mediziner. Dornach 2006, p. 141-154.

53 Cf. Peter Selg: Rudolf Steiner und die Freie Hochschule für Geisteswissenschaft. Die Begründung der "Ersten Klasse." Arlesheim 2008, p. 32ff.

54 Rudolf Steiner: Esoterische Unterweisungen für die erste Klasse der Freien Hochschule für Geisteswissenschaft am Goetheanum. Dornach 1992, GA 270c, p. 12.

55 Rudolf Steiner: Die Konstitution der Allgemeinen Anthroposophischen Gesellschaft und der Freien Hochschule für Geisteswissenschaft. (The Foundation Stone. RSP 1996). GA 260a, p. 172.

56 Ibid, p. 175.

57 Ibid, p. 358.

58 Ibid, p. 358.

59 Peter Selg: "Die Medizin muss Ernst machen mit dem geistigen Leben." Rudolf Steiners Hochschulkurse für die jungen Mediziner. Dornach 2006.

60 Rudolf Steiner: Esoterische Unterweisungen für die erste Klasse der Freien Hochschule für Geisteswissenschaft am Goetheanum. GA 270a, p. 149.

61 Cf.: Peter Selg: "Von der Beziehung zur Hochschule – Lehrer, Ärzte und Priester im Jahre 1924." In: the newssheet of the weekly Das Goetheanum, No. 50, 2010, p. 1-4.

62 Rudolf Steiner: Die Weltgeschichte in anthroposophischer Beleuchtung. (World History. RSP 1977). GA 233, p. 153.

63 Rudolf Steiner: Die Weihnachtstagung zur Begründung der Allgemeinen Anthroposophischen Gesellschaft 1923/24. (The Christmas Conference. AP 1990). GA 260, p. 284; author's emphasis.

64 Rudolf Steiner: Die Konstitution der Allgemeinen Anthroposophischen Gesellschaft und der Freien Hochschule für Geisteswissenschaft. (The Foundation Stone. RSP 1996). GA 260a, p. 60.

65   Cf. Peter Selg: "Zur Entstehung des Buches Grundlegendes zu einer Erweiterung der Heilkunst nach geisteswissen-schaftlichen Erkenntnissen." In: Peter Selg (ed.): *Und in der Tat, dies wirkte.*" *Die Krankengeschichten des Buches "Grundlegendes für eine Erweiterung der Heilkunst nach geisteswissenschaftlichen Erkenntnissen" von Rudolf Steiner und Ita Wegman. Eine Dokumentation.* Dornach 2007.

66   Rudolf Steiner: *Die Konstitution der Allgemeinen Anthroposophischen Gesellschaft und der Freien Hochschule für Geisteswissenschaft. (The Foundation Stone.* RSP 1996). GA 260a, p. 489.

67   Rudolf Steiner: *Die Weihnachtstagung zur Begründung der Allgemeinen Anthroposophischen Gesellschaft 1923/24. (The Christmas Conference.* AP 1990). GA 260, p. 212f.

68   Ibid, p. 52.

69   Rudolf Steiner: *Die Konstitution der Allgemeinen Anthroposophischen Gesellschaft und der Freien Hochschule für Geisteswissenschaft. (The Foundation Stone.* RSP 1996). GA 260a, p. 99.

70   Cf. Peter Selg: *Rudolf Steiners Toten-Gedenken. Die Verstorbenen, der Dornacher Bau und die Anthroposophische Gesellschaft. (The Path of the Soul after Death.* SteinerBooks 2011). Arlesheim 2008.

71   Cf. Peter Selg: *Rudolf Steiner und die Freie Hochschule für Geisteswissenschaft. Die Begründung der «Ersten Klasse».* Arlesheim 2008.

72   Cf. Peter Selg: *Elisabeth Vreede, 1879–1943.* Arlesheim 2009, p. 148 ff.

73   Siegfried Pickert, for instance—one of the pioneers of anthroposophic curative education—tells of the shock caused by the death of Rudolf Steiner and the uncertain fate of the "Lauenstein," which had been successfully founded shortly before; he then goes on to say: "That things continued is due to Ita Wegman. [...] sustained by youthful activity, already at Whitsun of the same year [1925], a great, mighty Whitsun conference was held. Ita Wegman gave the whole, driving impetus for this, in association with other executive council

friends. At this 1925 Whitsun conference further important developments occurred for curative education work. We were able to tell Ita Wegman how things were looking where we were. She absorbed all this with the profoundest interest, giving her young visitors the clear, tangible impression in the depths of their souls that the strength of Rudolf Steiner is now active in and through Ita Wegman." In Peter Selg: *Der Engel über dem Lauenstein. Siegfried Pickert, Ita Wegman und die Heilpädagogik.* Dornach 2004, p. 57.

74 "Nothing more interesting than this unsurpassed performance. Nothing more moving than the interior organization of this group animated by artistic faith." Quoted in Edwin Froböse (ed.): *Marie Steiner. Ihr Weg zur Erneuerung der Bühnenkunst durch die Anthroposophie.* Dornach 1973, p. 218.

75 Rudolf Steiner: *Perspektiven der Menschheitsentwickelung.* (*Materialism and the Task of Anthroposophy.* Anthroposophic Press 1987). GA 204. Dornach 1979, p. 106.

76 Minutes of the 1935 annual general meeting, Archive at the Goetheanum. In: Peter Selg: *Geistiger Widerstand und Überwindung. Ita Wegman 1933–1935.* Dornach 2005, p. 86.

77 Rudolf Steiner: *Anthroposophische Menschenerkenntnis und Medizin.* (*The Healing Process.* SteinerBooks 2000). GA 319. Dornach 1982, p. 220.

78 Rudolf Steiner: *Das Schicksalsjahr 1923 in der Geschichte der Anthroposophischen Gesellschaft.* GA 259, p. 254.

79 Cf. Peter Selg: *Elisabeth Vreede, 1879–1943*, p. 113f.

80 Address in Dornach, September 19, 1914. In: *Rudolf Steiner: Schicksalszeichen auf dem Entwickelungswege der Anthroposophischen Gesellschaft.* Ed. Marie Steiner. Dornach 1943, p. 37.

81 Rudolf Steiner: *Das Schicksalsjahr 1923 in der Geschichte der Anthroposophischen Gesellschaft.* GA 259, p. 344.

82 Gerhard Kienle: "Proposal for reform of the Medical Section." Typescript 1976. Kienle's whole text reads as follows: "Reform and reconfiguration of the whole medical movement is urgently needed. Conditions among physicians are tense, not only in a personal and psychological sense

but also in regard to matters of fundamental principle. One group within anthroposophic medicine regards natural medical approaches such as homeopathy, acupuncture, electroacupuncture, etc., as procedures that might bear fruit in future with the help of anthroposophic perspectives, and therefore does not regard their use as fundamentally objectionable in the context of anthroposophic medical practice. For example, Weleda uses electro-acupuncture procedures to monitor quality and shelf-life of its medicines. Another group, in contrast, believes that the only fruitful future path for medicine is based on Rudolf Steiner's medical courses. Representatives of this clinical tendency see natural healing methods as an atavistic throwback. The use of so-called 'image-forming' methods in diagnosis—such as the crystallization test and the 'rising image'—is regarded by many as a path whereby anthroposophy can imbue medicine, whereas others see diagnostic use of such methods as intensification of the materialistic errors of orthodox medicine. These disagreements are not resolved. Thus our medical approach lacks a unifying, spiritual character, which in turn impacts negatively on the widespread spiritual and legal conflicts in which our medical movement lives today. This situation is exacerbated by organizational difficulties. The anthroposophic movement, the medical section in particular, has only a very small number of really active and productive members. The current forms of organization lead to excessive numbers of meetings and gatherings at which, basically, the same issues are repeatedly discussed since the differing composition of committees requires continual repetition. Not only does this prevent dealing adequately with decisive issues; but it also hinders leading individuals from drawing fully and fruitfully on their capacities on behalf of the overall movement. The many meetings frequently prevent them from working on the spiritual form and configuration of the medical movement.

A further obstacle is the excessive number of people sitting on leadership committees. A group of 2 to 3 people can still hold a phone conversation together, whereas any additional people render communication more difficult. With growing numbers, meetings become necessary instead of communication by phone or letter. The length of meetings also grows disproportionately.

On the other hand, almost all leadership committees in the anthroposophic movement have the problem that they are also composed of individuals who are no longer actively involved in the field, but who put forward their personal points of view and wish to be heard. Members who are still actively working, who usually have differentiated professional knowledge and evaluative capacity, usually need much less time to discuss the necessary decisions. Active, younger members find it very difficult to join these leadership committees.

I would therefore like to propose a concept for re-organizing the medical movement.

The section leadership:

The section leadership should consist of 1 to 3 members. A section director should be chosen to have a kind of cabinet-forming role and select the other members, who must then be confirmed by the executive council. Individuals who are section leaders must be able to represent the medical movement both internally and publicly, and must also distinguish themselves through their own accomplishments. They must also be able to assess which physicians bring to expression a spiritual leadership in the medical movement. In other words, they must be able to evaluate the achievements and productivity of individuals. Furthermore, they must be able to at least approximately judge the significance of specialist medical issues for humanity, to grasp overall contexts, and to plan and implement long-term projects. They must also be able not only to engender their own spiritual work, but also to integrate that of others into an overall framework and bring it to fruition. They must not shy away from making and taking responsibility for decisions of major scope and importance. The section leadership determines its own rules of procedure. There is no need for it to be based in Dornach.

It is conceivable that tasks can be distributed—e.g. responsibility for work in various countries. The section leaders can have assistants who work on their behalf. The section leader should be supported by a section manager based in Dornach, whose task involves communicating, organizing, and coordinating conferences, meetings, etc. If the rules of procedure do not state otherwise, the section manager would initially be assigned to the Section leadership chairperson.

The section collegium:
The section collegium would comprise the actual representatives of different groups in local areas and fields of expertise. They would meet to inform one another about processes, problems, and tasks, and together elaborate with the section leadership the overall planning and coordination for different groups. The members of the section collegium acquaint the section leadership with problems arising in their areas sufficiently to enable resulting questions to be specifically discussed and resolved, as far as possible, in the section gatherings. The members of the section collegium should also ensure that the work of individuals active in the different groupings also bears fruit for the other members of the Medical Section.

Schooling and scientific study within the section should be actively supported by all productive individuals. Insofar as members of the section collegium represent legally autonomous institutions, they form an umbrella association chaired by at least one member of the section leadership. This umbrella association could, for example, be the current IAV [International Association of Physicians].

The esoteric group of physicians:
This should focus on its original task of publicly representing the intentions of the Medical Section. Only the leadership of the Medical Section should admit members to this group. This group would carry and realize a major part of the work of the Medical Section.
(In: Peter Selg: *Gerhard Kienle. Leben und Werk.* Vol. I. Dornach 2003, p. 736 f.).

83 Rudolf Steiner: *Die Konstitution der Allgemeinen Anthroposophischen Gesellschaft und der Freien Hochschule für Geisteswissenschaft.* (*The Foundation Stone.* RSP 1996). GA 260a, p. 441.

84 In relation to the still unclarified historical question as to whether Rudolf Steiner originally envisioned appointing the leader of the Fine Arts Section, Edith Maryon—who had fallen ill—to the executive council, see Rex Raab: *Edith Maryon. Bildhauerin und Mitarbeiterin Rudolf Steiners.* Dornach 1993, p. 362.

85 Rudolf Steiner: *Die Konstitution der Allgemeinen Anthroposophischen Gesellschaft und der Freien Hochschule für Geisteswissenschaft.* (*The Foundation Stone.* RSP 1996). GA 260a, p. 485.

86 Ibid, p. 238.

87 Rudolf Steiner: *Das Schicksalsjahr 1923 in der Geschichte der Anthroposophischen Gesellschaft.* GA 259, p. 330.

88 Rudolf Steiner: *Die Konstitution der Allgemeinen Anthroposophischen Gesellschaft und der Freien Hochschule für Geisteswissenschaft.* (*The Foundation Stone.* RSP 1996). GA 260a, p. 105.

89 Ibid, p. 77 f.

90 Ibid, p. 104.

91 Rudolf Steiner: *Das Schicksalsjahr 1923 in der Geschichte der Anthroposophischen Gesellschaft.* GA 259, p. 298.

92 Cf. Peter Selg: *Albert Steffen. Begegnung mit Rudolf Steiner.* Dornach 2009, p. 110 ff.

93 Rudolf Steiner: *Die Konstitution der Allgemeinen Anthroposophischen Gesellschaft und der Freien Hochschule für Geisteswissenschaft.* (*The Foundation Stone.* RSP 1990). GA 260a, p. 92.

94 Rudolf Steiner: *Zur Geschichte und aus den Inhalten der ersten Abteilung der Esoterischen Schule 1904-1914.* (*From the History and Contents of the First Section of the Esoteric School. Letters, Documents, and Lectures: 1904-1914.* SteinerBooks 2010). GA 264. Dornach 1996, p. 431.

95 Ibid.

96   Rudolf Steiner: *Das Schicksalsjahr 1923 in der Geschichte der Anthroposophischen Gesellschaft.* GA 259, p. 75.

97   Cf. Peter Selg: *Willem Zeylmans van Emmichoven. Anthroposophie und Anthroposophische Gesellschaft im 20. Jahrhundert.* Arlesheim 2009.

98   Rudolf Steiner: *Wege zu einem neuen Baustil.* (*Architecture as a Synthesis of the Arts.* Rudolf Steiner Press 1999). GA 286. Dornach 1982, p. 62.

99   Rudolf Steiner: *Das Schicksalsjahr 1923 in der Geschichte der Anthroposophischen Gesellschaft.* GA 259, p. 683.

100 Rudolf Steiner: *Die Konstitution der Allgemeinen Anthroposophischen Gesellschaft und der Freien Hochschule für Geisteswissenschaft.* (*The Foundation Stone.* RSP 1996). GA 260a, p. 99.

101 Rudolf Steiner: *Mysterienstätten des Mittelalters.* GA 233a. (*Rosicrucianism and Modern Initiation.* Rudolf Steiner Press 1982). Dornach 1991, p. 135.

102 *Esoterische Unterweisungen für die erste Klasse der Freien Hochschule für Geisteswissenschaft am Goetheanum.* GA 270b, p. 31.

103 Michael Bauer: *Gesammelte Werke.* Vol. 5. Ed. Christoph Rau. Stuttgart 1997, p. 40 f.

Books by Peter Selg

THE AGRICULTURE COURSE, KOBERWITZ, WHITSUN 1924
Rudolf Steiner and the Beginnings of Biodynamics
Floris Books 2005

THE CHILD WITH SPECIAL NEEDS
Letters and Essays on Curative Education
Floris Books 2009

CHRIST AND THE DISCIPLES
The Destiny of an Inner Community
SteinerBooks November 2011

THE CREATIVE POWER OF ANTHROPOSOPHICAL CHRISTOLOGY
SteinerBooks November 2011

THE ESSENCE OF WALDORF EDUCATION
SteinerBooks 2010

THE FIGURE OF CHRIST
*Rudolf Steiner and the Spiritual Intention behind
the Goetheanum's Central Work of Art*
Temple Lodge 2009

THE FUNDAMENTAL SOCIAL LAW
*Rudolf Steiner on the Work of the Individual
and the Spirit of Community*
SteinerBooks October 2011

A GRAND METAMORPHOSIS
*Contributions to the Spiritual-Scientific Anthropology
and Education of Adolescents*
SteinerBooks 2008

ITA WEGMAN AND KARL KÖNIG
Letters and Documents
Floris Books 2009

Karl König's Path to Anthroposophy
Floris Books 2008

Karl König: My Task
Autobiography and Biographies
Floris Books 2008

The Path of the Soul after Death
The Community of the Living and the Dead as Witnessed by
Rudolf Steiner in his Eulogies and Farewell Addresses
SteinerBooks 2011

Rudolf Steiner and the Fifth Gospel
Insights into a New Understanding of the Christ Mystery
SteinerBooks 2010

Rudolf Steiner as a Spiritual Teacher
From Recollections of Those Who Knew Him
SteinerBooks 2010

Rudolf Steiner's Intentions for the Anthroposophical
Society
The Executive Council, the School for Spiritual Science, and the Sections
SteinerBooks 2011

Seeing Christ in Sickness and Healing
Floris Books 2005

The Therapeutic Eye
How Rudolf Steiner Observed Children
SteinerBooks 2008

Unbornness
Human Pre-existence and the Journey toward Birth
SteinerBooks 2010

Ita Wegman Institute
for Basic Research into Anthroposophy
PFEFFINGER WEG 1 A CH-4144 ARLESHEIM, SWITZERLAND
www.wegmaninstitut.ch
e-mail: sekretariat@wegmaninstitut.ch

The Ita Wegman Institute for Basic Research into Anthroposophy is a non-profit research and teaching organization. It undertakes basic research into the lifework of Dr. Rudolf Steiner (1861–1925) and the application of Anthroposophy in specific areas of life, especially medicine, education, and curative education. Work carried out by the Institute is supported by a number of foundations and organizations and an international group of friends and supporters. The Director of the Institute is Prof. Dr. Peter Selg.

www.ingramcontent.com/pod-product-compliance
Lightning Source LLC
Chambersburg PA
CBHW020948090426
42736CB00010B/1324